my mom is a fob

MY mom IS A fob

earnest advice
in broken english
from your
asian-american mom

teresa wu
AND
serena wu

a perigee book

A PERIGEE BOOK
Published by the Penguin Group
Penguin Group (USA) Inc.
375 Hudson Street, New York, New York 10014, USA

Penguin Group (Canada), 90 Eglinton Avenue East, Suite 700, Toronto, Ontario M4P 2Y3, Canada
(a division of Pearson Penguin Canada Inc.)
Penguin Books Ltd., 80 Strand, London WC2R 0RL, England
Penguin Group Ireland, 25 St. Stephen's Green, Dublin 2, Ireland (a division of Penguin Books Ltd.)
Penguin Group (Australia), 250 Camberwell Road, Camberwell, Victoria 3124, Australia
(a division of Pearson Australia Group Pty. Ltd.)
Penguin Books India Pvt. Ltd., 11 Community Centre, Panchsheel Park, New Delhi—110 017, India
Penguin Group (NZ), 67 Apollo Drive, Rosedale, North Shore 0632, New Zealand
(a division of Pearson New Zealand Ltd.)
Penguin Books (South Africa) (Pty.) Ltd., 24 Sturdee Avenue, Rosebank,
Johannesburg 2196, South Africa
Penguin Books Ltd., Registered Offices: 80 Strand, London WC2R 0RL, England

While the author has made every effort to provide accurate telephone numbers and Internet addresses
at the time of publication, neither the publisher nor the author assumes any responsibility for errors
or for changes that occur after publication. Further, the publisher does not have any control over and
does not assume any responsibility for author or third-party websites or their content.

First edition: January 2011

Library of Congress Cataloging-in-Publication Data

Wu, Teresa.
  My mom is a fob : earnest advice in broken English from your Asian-American mom /
Teresa Wu and Serena Wu.— 1st ed.
    p.   cm.
  ISBN 978-0-399-53640-3
  1. Mothers—Humor.   2. Asian Americans—Humor.   3. English language—Humor.
  4. Mothers—Quotations.   I. Wu, Serena.   II. Title.
  PN6231.M68W85 2011
  818.'607—dc22   2010035139

PRINTED IN THE UNITED STATES OF AMERICA

10   9   8   7   6   5   4   3   2   1

Most Perigee books are available at special quantity discounts for bulk purchases for sales promotions,
premiums, fund-raising, or educational use. Special books, or book excerpts, can also be created to
fit specific needs. For details, write: Special Markets, Penguin Group (USA) Inc., 375 Hudson Street,
New York, New York 10014.

For Maree Wu and Yina Wu,
our beloved 媽媽s.

CONTENTS

MARGARET CHO

My mom is a fob. But my dad is not. This is because when I was three days old, my father was deported. This was very traumatic for my parents and for me in particular. My parents were forced to put a nearly just-born me on a plane in the care of flight attendants—then called "stewardesses"—so that my father and his family could care for me in Korea as my mother stayed in the United States to make money and try to figure out a way to get her family back. My mother still cries when she thinks about putting me into the arms of these strange women in uniforms. "Can you imagine? This kind of thing? So terrible! Can you believe? So hard for Mommy. Wha!"

Since I was actually born in the United States, my Americanness was never taken for granted, and when my father was later allowed back into the country, when I was about three years old, he did everything he could to make sure what had happened would never happen again. It was his personal project to rid himself of any fob tendencies. He had no discernable accent. If anything, people thought he might be from the East Coast. Once when I was a bit older, I was going to stay overnight at a friend's house and this friend's mother had called and spoken to my father on the phone. When I arrived, she asked me if I was adopted. I said that I wasn't, and she said, "Well, that is strange because I just spoke to your daddy and he is clearly Uh-merican. Plain as day." He'd taken on an American name. Instead of Cho Seung Hoon, he told people to call him Joe. "Hey, Joe."

And as I was the only legitimate American citizen in my whole giant extended Korean family, they all took great pains to ensure my Americanness. I was the American who was going to help them out. I was America to them. My parents both spoke Korean to me, but I was not allowed to speak back to them in Korean. I had to answer in perfect English. And even that wasn't good enough sometimes. My father worked for an insurance company, and there was a publication put out by the firm that featured the writing of different employees' children. My father submitted a piece that he had written himself with my photograph attached, signing my name to it. It was a recipe of sorts for bulgogi, a very typical Korean meat dish served in our household. In it he used a bizarre baby language that he had invented for me. It was something to the effect of "My mommy uses her magic fingers to make the meat taste so good." I believe that the title of the story was "Magic Fingers." I was so horrified when I read it and so incredibly embarrassed that it was published under my name. I may have been only about five years old at the time, yet I still felt I had an image to protect. I asked him why he had done that, but he just changed the subject. But I have a feeling that he thought whatever I would have written wouldn't have been American enough.

My father's fight against fobbishness made my mother's fob tendencies bloom in full. We always had food that had eyes—big sheets of tiny dried fish stuck together, black eyes covering the surface like poppy seeds. Tentacles were always coming out of someone's mouth. We had multiple refrigerators, some broken, some working—all with big jars of kimchi in various stages of decay. Our house smelled so bad, but you would think that Bing Crosby was living there, from the way my father would smoke his pipe and pick up the phone to say, "Hello?" I used to be very embarrassed by my mother's fob life and the way she would say, "Let's go to MON-GOH-MERRY U-Ward-uh!" referring to the then popular department store Montgomery Ward. I wanted to be white so badly then, but it never happened, so I dreamed better and bigger dreams—like becoming a comedian.

When I started doing comedy, I naturally gravitated toward making jokes about my mother, and the fact that she was a fob, because I had been making fun of her for so long. It was what I knew. I think that if you are Asian American, making

fun of your mom being a fob is a rite of passage, a way to sepa-
rate yourself from your family. A way to say, I am not them.
I still love them, and I am still grateful, but I am not them. I
love *My Mom Is a Fob* because it captures the spirit of who
I was, who I am, and who I am in relation to my family. We
can share what happened to us. We can laugh and cry. We can
see we are truly American. And fuck that magic fingers shit.

TERESA WU

Ever had your mom ask you if you wanted a mushroom and spinach "helmet" for breakfast?

Your mom may in fact be a fob.

What *is* a fob exactly, you ask?

The acronym F.O.B. stands for "fresh off the boat," and is a term often used to describe Asian immigrants who just aren't quite on track with American culture. You know, if your family still eats Peking duck instead of turkey on Thanksgiving, owns a giant cleaver, and takes 24 more napkins than you need at Chipotle? That's fob status—and for the record, we aren't ashamed.

Though "F.O.B." was once a derogatory term, we like to think that we've seized ownership of it. In our minds, it's no longer an acronym; it's a word unto itself—fob. More important, it's no longer a slur. It's defined by our pride in having held on steadfastly to our half-Asian, half-American culture.

As the daughters of Taiwanese-American transplants, the two of us spent our childhood years in the bubble of the Asian suburbia that is Fremont, California. And so we grew up in a world where the "Little Taipei" strip mall was a freeway exit away, our brown-bag lunches regularly offered up red bean buns instead of PB&Js, and our PTA newsletters arrived in English on one side, Mandarin on the other.

Sure, as Asian Americans the two of us are technically a minority—but we've never been *in* the minority. With a 75 percent Asian student body, our high school was, as one might expect, a hotbed of National Science Bowl nerds. In some ways, the two of us fulfill all the Asian stereotypes you can think of. No, our mothers aren't that great of drivers, and yes, we did excel at musical instruments. We knock back pearl milk tea like it's Diet Coke, and we rocked the SATs— according to everybody's standards but our moms', anyway. In an environment in which being Asian was the rule, not the exception, there was never any discomfort nor any shame in having a funny-sounding last name or having your house smell like incense. It was easy to embrace our fobbiness, given that our community was full of it.

In calling our mothers "fobs," we're not trying to make fun of our moms—we think they're freakin' adorable, and we want to showcase those precious moments to a community of Asian-American kids who know exactly what it's like to be on the receiving end of that amazing, unconditional, and sometimes misspelled love. We heart our moms for everything they are: grammatical atrocities, awkward sex talks, and all.

These are the stories of kids just like us: first-generation American children of Asian immigrant parents. This book is about our Asian mothers who refuse to get in the car without their sun-protective arm sheaths. The ones who leave desperate voicemails asking us to "Please pick up phone? Hello? Are you there?" It's about the moms who open our STD test results, send us passive-aggressive text messages "from the dog" in hopes that we'll call home, and email us unsolicited advice about everything from homosexuality to constipation.

We hope you read these anecdotes, which have been submitted by our awesome blog readers, and laugh, cry, or—if you're lucky like us—find solace in the fact that thousands of moms out there are as painfully nosy, unintentionally hilarious, and endearingly fobby as yours is.

EMAILS FROM MY MOTHER

TERESA WU

As a blogger since the beginning of time, I've been posting snippets and snapshots of life with my fobby mom for as long as I can remember. In the fall of 2008, I strung together a series of our emails and Skype exchanges for a creative nonfiction class. It later went on to become the inspiration behind our blog and then this book.

I'd had it in the back of my head for a while to start a blog documenting my mother's hilarity (trust me, there was a lot of it)—and I mentioned it to Serena, who loved the concept. As they say—the rest was history. We created the website mymomisafob.com around midnight on October 18, 2008. While normal college kids embarked on the search for socially acceptable forms of Friday-night activity, the two of us went buck wild on, um, Tumblr, posting the cream of the crop from our repository of fobby mom emails.

While we were basically slapping our knees with laughter in front of our respective laptops, we weren't totally sure other people would sing the same tune. In fact, after attempting to solicit submissions from our friends at 1:26:57 a.m., we had a moment of desperation. I quote:

TERESA: WHY ISNT ANYONE SENDING US ANYTHING?

Uh, because you started the blog less than two hours ago, genius.

Five days later, with the help of chuckling Asian-American kids across the nation and all over the interwebs, our traffic exploded.

This is the story that started it all.

In my freshman year of college in San Diego, I made my mother a Gmail account and our relationship has, to be frank, never been the same.

October 1, 2007

Dear Mei Mei

How is weekend? Is everything ok?
    I look LV's website I found out one handbag It look nice. here Can you look it ,See what your suggestion. I am so suprise, Mark said he want to buy LV bags for

chrismas gifts, How nice brother he is. Anyway I am very
happy, he can think both of us.

Take care.

Love you
Mom

Is her space bar broken maybe? Since when does she know
how to link something? The next time I see her, she might
whip out CTRL+C or, God forbid, ALT+TAB. Looks like I'm
getting a bag for Christmas. Woo-wee. I am *very* happy my
brother can "think both of us," too.

October 8, 2007

Dear Mei,

How is you everything?

if Jessica askwhere I buy the paint (in kitchen), you
just told her you forget it. i don't want they buy same
paint as me.

Do you see mark's passport? he can't find it at
school, i can't find it in our house too.

take care

Love you
Mom

I guess having the same eggplant-shaded kitchen could be unfortunate. And it is a somewhat more legitimate concern than the time she told me not to tell Jessica where she bought her napkin holder. I mean, if all our kitchen décor started looking the same as Jessica's, our family friends might, you know, *judge* us.

. . . And they wonder where I get my silly jealousy complex from.

The next week, San Diego catches fire. I tell her I'm coming home.

October 22, 2007

DEAR MEI, OK
   I LOVE TO YOU? BUT HOW COME YOU COME
HOME? TAKE PLANE OR SOMETHING? EXPENSIVE!
MOM

Hmm, clearly I'm unwanted at home. Despite what one might interPRET AS CONCERN, SHE HAS REALLY JUST ACCIDENTALLY HIT CAPS LOCK.

I tell her that our RA has instructed us not to leave our apartments unless absolutely necessary. Several hours later, a concerned mother's afterthought arrives via my inbox:

October 22, 2007

if you can't go out how can you guys eat?

Mom

November 16, 2007

Dear Mei,

How are you? i didn't see you on line for past two days, Is everything ok? Midterm is finished, you can go to sleep for all weekend.and prepare to see you lovly Mom on Thanksgive Day.

Love & miss You
Mom

It was my birthday weekend, Mom. If you had talked to me online, it would have gone something like HIMAFMAH-HIHIHII MAMAMA!!! LOVE YOU! LOVELOVE LVOE! DRUNKZIEIEEE SDFJKLJDSFLKJ!!!!!

It is almost Chinese New Year. I think this is the first time I've celebrated Chinese New Year without my family and our seven-course feast. As always, my mom knows exactly how to make me feel at home.

February 2, 2008

Dear Mei,

For Rice cake you need material as below

(1) Rice cake powder-you can buy it on Ranch 99 is made in Japan,it's white box and print blue letter on it

(2) 3 eggs

(3) milk 3 cups

(4) 1.5 cup sugar

(5) 1tsp baking soda

(6) butter 1/2 cup

you can beat eggs first and melt butter then put all material together, mixed it untiil it smoth thenpre heat oven 375 cocked about 50 mimutes, use toothstick or folk to put in ,if nothing with it then it's done

enjoy it

love you

Wish you have happy chinese new year and whole year lucky and happy and health.

Mom

(She is either slightly dyslexic or extremely fobby. I'm 99 percent positive it's the latter. Try the recipe, I promise it's delicious. But don't *cock* anything while you're at it.)

February 11, 2008

Dear Mei,

How are you? I didn't see you in Skpye on past two days, is everything fine?

I will be leave Bali this morning amd arrival on Taipei around 7:00 PM, I will try to spyke you on line if you open your computer. Conrad Hotel is similar with Shronton I lived before, It's very nice, yesterday we went to Rizt Carton to do water spa, it's very good I told Dad i will bring you and mark with us vext and we will live in Rizt Caton, It's very beauity hotel, you will love it, but they don't have beach connect with hotel. in anyway we have very good vacation with Bali Island. talk you later.

Bye
Mom

I think being overseas throws off not only her internal clock but also her finger aim. She will try to "spyke" me online. That doesn't sound very safe. And, ha, they had a "good vacation with Bali Island" . . . as if the island participated in the fun. (How do her real estate clients understand?)

Sometimes, she gets a little needy. Just a tad, you know? But what good mother doesn't?

April 1, 2008

MEI, ARE YOU IN YOU APRTMENT!!!!

MOM

. . . So I taught her how to chat online. We're in a whole new e-world of fun now.

April 7, 2008

MOM:	Dear Mei,
TERESA:	what's up
MOM:	I got you credit card statement it's 197.78, Oh a lot
TERESA:	sorry . . . I had expensive books this quarter
MOM:	also you eat a lot too
TERESA:	sorry

TERESA: will eat less

MOM: how is your interview?

TERESA: good i think

MOM: only one person talk to you?

TERESA: yea

MOM: what's question he ask? or she

TERESA: ummmm just the same old stuff

MOM: is girl or boy

TERESA: girl

MOM: younger or older

TERESA: why so many questions???

MOM: nothing just boar

TERESA: bored** not boar

MOM: ok good night, my sweet heart, love you

Good night, Mom. Love you, too.

SOCIAL MEDIA LOVE

SERENA WU

My mom genuinely believes that her short stint in web 1.0 before the bubble burst qualifies her as a "l33t h4x0r"—a legitimate hacker well-versed in Internet Speak and social media tools. And while my sister and I are both old enough for her not to be a baby-cooing mommy blogger, she still misspells 140-character updates on Twitter.

> **Plan to visit grandpa's and granduncle's near Shanghai. While in oversea,if possible, learn to cook some international cousins as well.** ☆
>
> 10:16 PM Oct 7th, 2009 from web   ↰ Reply ⇄ Retweet

Considering that my grandpas and great-uncles are all in Taiwan and hers are long gone, she probably meant "elderly folks" (in nonpossessive form, with much respect). Rest assured, she's also not into cannibalism, but international cuisine.

It probably comes as no surprise that we're also friends on

Facebook—with wall restrictions. Her only alternative is to write on my dad's wall instead:

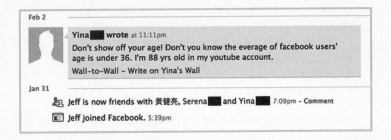

I'm sure the "everage" user on YouTube doesn't lie about her age either, nor does she send her kids video links of TED talks and university lectures for personal enrichment. I get quite a few of those.

Despite our awkward e-lationship (where she plays online predator and I become stalked prey), I still appreciate her genuine efforts to understand and connect with me when in-person communication is not possible.

My mom's the determined yet humble type who always places my sister and me first and her life second. When I was in kindergarten, my mom would drive me to a private school in the morning then a public school in the afternoon, followed by joint violin lessons at a friend's house. She'd make me practice until my fingers blistered, bandage every fingertip carefully so that I could still press down on the strings accurately, and then have me practice some more at home while she accompanied on the piano. It's a pity that I no longer remember how to play.

In elementary school, my mom dragged me out of bed at 5:30 in the morning to go ice skating before class started while she played multiplication rap in the car. By junior high, she was sending me to after-school math tutoring because a B was unacceptable. Come high school, SAT prep classes were mandatory, not an option. Once I got to college, she pressured me to switch out of architecture and go into engineering (though without any success).

It makes sense, then, that after college, my mom still assigns me homework . . . via Twitter:

> **@serenawu weekly oral report due 11:59 pm ea Sun. What you've learned/sensed both explicit/ tacit knowledg & how this may affect you/action** ☆
>
> 9:30 PM Feb 6th from web in reply to serenawu   ↩ Reply ↻ Retweet

. . . tough love.

While this book is a compilation of all of those Gchat conversations, Facebook wall-to-walls, cryptic cell phone texts, and more, each misspelled statement of love reveals something to be cherished—be it the outlandish gestures or genuine concerns.

In a way, the overarching story to be told is that of our immigrant parents raising us, the first generation, in a world apart from theirs where cultural and language barriers make day-to-day communication a challenge and mutual understanding a lifelong learning process. My mom's efforts do not go unnoticed nor do I feel alone in my experiences. At some point, you'll probably think to yourself, "My mom does that, too," and we'll have accomplished something meaningful: showing you that there is nothing to be embarrassed or frustrated about. We are all embracing a fobby generation together—with a bit of patience and a lot of laughter.

my mom is a fob

CHAPTER ONE

fob fashion

Fob mothers have a rather particular taste in fashion, to say the least. Be it a giant plastic visor for an evening stroll or strangely patterned protective arm covers for a five-minute drive, our moms have seamlessly integrated truly iconic pieces into their daily wardrobes. Somehow, some way, our fob mothers have branded their own signature looks without the help of Stacy and Clinton—and probably on a flea market budget, no less. While their giant sun-shading umbrellas may not be the chicest parasols around, they sure are major head-turners on clear days at the park. You've probably also borne witness to the sight that is a small Asian lady toting a personal, compact shopping cart behind her, crossing the street at a snail's pace, with the vegetables overstuffing her method of grocery transport in mortal peril. Forget Lady Gaga—we'd argue that in the realm of inexplicably fearless couture, fob mothers take front and center.

Here are a few pointers on how to look just like a fob mom:

- Curly perm

- Jade bracelet

- Huge plastic visor

- Cloth arm covers

- Sunblock with an SPF nearing triple digits

- Face creams of questionable origin, color, and texture

- Stirrup pants

- Sheer nude pantyhose, worn with said stirrup pants

And here's a small sample of our cute mothers:

fob mom head gear

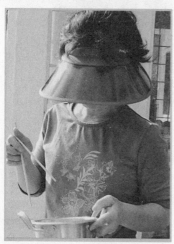

uv protection

multipurpose protective sleeves

tourist fashion

her idea, not mine

dirty t-shirt

My mom is gardening outside . . .

ME:	Um. Mom, can I see the front of your T-shirt?
ME:	Oh my god. That says "10 Reasons Why Beer Is Better Than Women." You can't wear that outside!
MOM:	It's good for getting dirty!

no need for long sucks

MOM:	Don't buy Mommy and Daddy Christmas presents this year. If anything, buy Dad some long suck. We don't need anything.
ME:	What's a long suck?
MOM:	The long suck is the dress suck. When you sit down, people would not see your skin. Which is both you and Daddy sometimes show you skin between suck and pant when sit down. There were so many photos of Daddy sitting on the stage with his skin showing, WOW. Not good. Longer suck is more expensive. Five dollars each or something

like that. Daddy just buy short sucks. You need get
one yourself when wear formal. My dear son especially, you want to be lawyer. Then dress like one.

retail misunderstanding

My mom sees a pair of stylishly ripped jeans at American
Eagle Outfitters and takes it to the cash register.

"These pants are ripped . . . can I get discount?"

CHAPTER TWO

communication
barriers

When English is your second language, it becomes difficult to remember exactly how to spell or pronounce words correctly— let alone differentiate between a verb and a noun. In light of our own bilingual ineptitude—so what if the only thing we're capable of in Chinese is ordering dim sum?—we give our moms major props for their incredible hurdles in learning an unfamiliar tongue. Naturally, not all of their English language lessons came from grammatically and phonetically rigorous textbooks: Our parents have spent the last several years picking up new vocabulary from the radio, the TV, and, hell, even the corner supermarket. With the utmost courage, our moms valiantly whip out their newly learned phrases on the regular.

Often in public earshot, we might add, despite never having learned the proper spelling for such phrases. See, fob mothers truly speak a foreign language of their own. To an outsider, this language sounds like a cacophony of mismatching verbiage, but in reality, it's a language spoken universally in Asian households across America. Because from the day our parents' generation set foot in the land of the free and the home of the brave, the most awesome language of all time was born: Engrish.

passed . . . what?!

My uncle had just gotten into a car accident—nothing too major, but he did lose consciousness at one point. Since his English isn't very good, he asked my mother to call his insurance company for him. My mother called them, and after explaining for the longest time why she was calling on his behalf, she started to tell them what happened . . .

> **MOM (said with no emotion whatsoever):** My brother was in accident today. Car hit him from behind. Not his fault. Because of accident, my brother passed away.
>
> **INSURANCE AGENT:** Passed away?! Um . . . I'm so sorry to hear that . . .
>
> **MOM:** Oh, ha-ha, sorry, sorry. I mean passed *out*.

potty mouth

Mom and I were talking about email accounts, and I noticed she was pronouncing the word "account" very carefully . . .

ME: Why are you pronouncing it like that?

MOM: People at work say I pronounce like bad word.

ME: What word?

MOM: I don't know.

ME: Well, how did you used to pronounce it?

MOM: "A-cunt."

ME: . . .

MOM: You know what word?

10-YEAR-OLD SISTER: Yeah, what word?

ME: Uh . . . I don't know, either?

dancing drums

MOM: Better to have kids young, otherwise they may get dancing drum.

ME: Wait, what?

MOM: Dancing drum! How can you not know dancing drum?!

ME: Down's syndrome . . . ?

more than silverware

We were at a restaurant, and my mom accidentally dropped her knife on the floor . . .

MOM: Hi, can I please get a new life? I dropped it.
WAITER: . . . A new life?

doing marianna

MOM: You know Marianna? You don't do it, right?
ME: Who is Marianna?
MOM: Marianna! You know! You don't do it, right?
ME: You mean marijuana?
MOM: Yes, Marianna!
ME: Maybe you should just call it "weed."

the best bitches are in california

My mom was telling people in Maryland about moving to California . . .

MOM: It's really great! There are lots of bitches there.

NEIGHBOR: Oh?

SISTER: Mom, it's pronounced *beaches.*

goober lady

I'm 27, and I was telling my mom about flirting with a 17-year-old . . .

MOM: hmm..you're a goober

ME: what>?>??? what's a goober

MOM: You know, old woman who chase young boy

ME: oh. a COUGAR?

MOM: yeah whatever.

a vulgar choice of restaurant

While we were deciding where to go to dinner . . .

"Hey, how about the Fuckruckers!"

the louder, the better

We were in the Philippines for a wedding, and family from all over was visiting. My aunt, who lives in Ireland, brought her Irish boyfriend, Quinn. My mom wanted to start a conversation, but she thought that Quinn didn't speak English . . .

> **MOM (shouting):** HELLO!
>
> **QUINN (mouth full):** Hello.
>
> **MOM:**   HOW ARE YOU?
>
> **QUINN:** Fine, thanks.
>
> **MOM:**   DO YOU KNOW WHAT YOU ARE EATING?
>
> **ME (aside to my cousin):** Why is she talking so loud?
>
> **COUSIN:** He speaks English. He's not deaf.

frickin' chicken

My mom brought over some KFC for a backyard barbecue . . .

"Hey, guys! Time for some Kentucky Frickin' Chicken!"

sit!

My friend's mom visited my house from Asia. She was trying to train my dog, Monday . . .

"Shit, Monday, shit!"

quban spelling

I overheard my mom trying to pay her credit card bill over the phone . . .

> **CREDIT CARD REPRESENTATIVE:** OK, can I have your reference number?
>
> **MOM (in a thick Filipino accent):** OK, yes. It's 221, B as in boy, A as in apple, 743, D as in Dog, and Q, Q as in Cuba.

hospitality gone wrong

When my mom stayed over at my grandparents' place for the first time after she and my dad got married, she wrote them a thank-you card . . .

Thank you for your hostility.

in search of shitty banks

My mom was visiting my fiancé's Caucasian mother in Arizona and didn't know the area.

MOM: Where is Shitty Bank?
FIANCÉ'S MOM (perplexed): Well, there are a lot of shitty
            banks here. Which one are you looking for?
MOM: Shitty Bank? Sheeeettty Bank? Seetty Bank?
FIANCÉ'S MOM: Oh, you mean Citibank?

fruity animals

MOM: I found a nice antelope and cut it up for you.

ME: Are you sure about that?

MOM: Antelope? No, no . . . not antelope . . . the other one . . . HONEYDEW!

sandwich bombs

ME: Hmm, there's a terrorist alert going on the subways in New York for the holidays.

MOM: Really? Well, you really shouldn't eat their sandwiches then.

caffeinated love child

BARISTA: Can I take your order, ma'am?

MOM (struggles quietly for a moment): Can I have a . . . crappuccino?

"playing" with the cat

After I got my new kitten, Kirby . . .

>   **MOM:**   What are you doing tonight?
>
>   **ME:**   Probably just staying in. I don't think I want to go
>   out.
>
>   **MOM:**   Good, good, that way you and Kirby can do some
>   bondage!

hanging suspicion

My older sister tried to expose what I did right before Thanksgiving weekend . . .

>   **SISTER:** So, how's your haaaaangoooover?
>
>   **ME:**   Shhhh! It's fine; I'm great. **(I give my older sister a
>   nasty look)**
>
>   **MOM:**   Who you hang with? What guy you hang with?
>   Who my little baby hang with?

bonus marriages

MOM (talking about a friend of hers): Her extra husband came to her house for Thanksgiving dinner.

ME: Ex-husband?

MOM: No, no, extra husband. She divorce and remarry, so she have extra one.

aromatic toilet water

MOM: Can you figure out how to use this toilet spray?

ME (looking at a purple bottle of Calvin Klein perfume): This is perfume . . .

MOM: It says it's toilet spray right on the box!

ME: Let me see the box.

(my mom hands me Calvin Klein box)

ME (reads "eau de toilette"): This is NOT toilet spray. *Eau de toilette* is French for perfume!

MOM: I was wondering why it came in such a pretty bottle.

angus's unfortunate renaming

Here's an excerpt from an email I received from my mom regarding my friend Angus . . .

> . . . and how is your friend Anus doing? I haven't seen him hang out with you in long while . . . hope Anus doing good!

hurting the testes

My mom was teaching me how to make fried rice over Gchat . . .

MOM: use ham,egg & pees, fry egg first and take out then put some more oil before fry rice, then put pees, ham, before take them out , put some diced green onion, smell better

ME: that sounds good . . . but lots of ingredients

MOM: I think you don't have to do it exactly, just omit the one you think is not going to hurt the teste

dirty designers

MOM: My friend gave me a coochie watch.

ME: Mom! Don't say that!

MOM: Why?

ME: You mean Gucci watch!

MOM: What is coochie?

serve well, children

My mom took out a bottle of Arbor Mist and started pouring it for the kids . . .

ME: What are you doing?!

MOM: Your aunt said kids can drink this one.

(I look at the bottle)

ME: It says serve well chilled, not serve well children.

sat vocabulary fail

My mom and I were watching the movie *The Phantom of the Opera* . . .

MOM (completely mesmerized): What's "seduction" mean?

ME (trying to act nonchalant): Uh . . .

MOM: Tsk! You get 2260 on SATs and you don't know?

meat mistake

KFC EMPLOYEE: Welcome to KFC. Can I take your order?

MOM: Yes, please, can I have one bucket of chicken?

KFC EMPLOYEE: Sure! White or dark meat, ma'am?

MOM: Duck!? I don't want duck! I want chicken!

the hat that dug and begged

My mom owned a fast-food restaurant, and on her to-buy list the following was written down . . .

Hat Dug Beg

I read it for awhile until I realized she wanted to buy "hot dog bags."

the petsmart abortion clinic

MOM: Excuse me, how much for abortion?

PETSMART EMPLOYEE (whispering): We don't do abortions here.

MOM: But I saw sign outside.

PETSMART EMPLOYEE: That's not abortion, that's adoption.

edible cosmetics

MOM: Why is in the bathroom? This should put in kitchen?

ME: Why would it be in the kitchen?

MOM: This is thing for eating.

ME: What?!

MOM: Look, it say "Bread Butter."

ME: No, Mom, it says "Beard Buster."

cereal and stds

ME: Mom, I know this guy, and he has sex with different girls all the time!

MOM: Ew! He should be careful. He could catch granola.

ME: What's granola?

MOM: You know—GRANOLA! The sex disease!

ME: You mean GONORRHEA?!

high on wallawalla

MOM: The people were so scary and they smelled really bad, like *da ma*.

ME: What's "da-ma"?

MOM: It's drugs!

ME: What kind of drug? There are lots of drugs.

MOM: Oh, it's malawala. Or wallawalla. One of those.

ME: . . . Marijuana?!

supersize that salad

WAITRESS: Soup or salad?

MOM: Yes, please.

ME: Mom, soup *or* salad. Not super salad.

MOM: Oh. Salad, please.

wild hogs vs. wild women

We were having a typical night watching TV before dinner. My mom came home from work and saw a wild hog on the screen.

MOM: Hey, it's a whore!

ME: . . . You mean a boar?

MOM: Ha-ha-ha-ha, right, boar. Oops! Good thing only you heard that.

sentence structure

My mom helpfully volunteered to tutor my little cousin . . .

MOM: Now spell "window."

COUSIN: Window? Give me a hint! A sentence!

MOM: Hmm, OK . . . "Window we go to church?"

lost on ventura bluebird

MOM: You take Ventura Bulu-bard, and left on Winnetka.

GUEST: I think I'm lost. I can't find Ventura Bluebird.

MOM: Not bluebird, BULU-BARD. B-L-V-D. Bulu-bard!

dad's hormonal changes

MOM: Your daddy is so moody these days. Sometime he angry, sometime he sad. That is why I say he's going through mental pause.

ME: Mom, it's called "menopause," not "mental pause."

MOM: Aye, you know what I mean.

touching you

Hi! Sandra,

yesterday a girl call Sophia from Nottingham gave me a ring. She wanted touch you,so I gave your email address. ok! take care.

Love Mum xxx

ready for halloween

I am in San Diego to haunt the house with your brother.

what a hell!

What time did you back to Apartment last night ? Did you go to work today? What a hell ! Anyway, it is not always happen, so, cheer up. How was check up the mri test. What Dr. said about your brain. Tomorrow, me and dad go to lunch, before it take walk at beech. freiday we are going to Nutt berry farm to see thanksgiving festivable. oh shopping too. It will be fun weekend.

Kristin we miss you. hope you have good weekend too. hug and kiss to you.

Bye.

hey, mr. dj

My mom had written "DJ Masta" on the notepad on the coffee table . . .

ME: What the hell? Who is DJ Masta?

MOM: Ohhh, I was watching a cooking show this afternoon, and they said to use that on sandwiches.

ME: You mean . . . dijon mustard?

getting the chills

MOM: Have you talked to your brother lately? Is he OK?

SISTER: I think so. I talked to him online the other day. He seems fine.

MOM: Oh, really? He emailed me and said he's chilling.

SISTER: Uhh . . . yeah, he's "chilling." You know, relaxing?

MOM: Oh, you mean he's not sick? He's not cold?

ahoy, matey!

ME: Do you remember Laura? She wants to be a pilot in the Air Force.

MOM: What?

ME: A pilot . . .

MOM (looking confused and thinking intensely): So . . . Laura wants to be . . . a pirate?

loling mom

From: Mom

Tommy how is mammoth? do you still have a cold?

—LOL mom.

From: Me

laughing out loud mom?

From: Mom

i thought it meant LOTS OF LOVE?

hey, grr-friend

MOM: Hey, grr!
ME: What?
MOM: I said, "Hey, grr!"
MOM: I hear young people say it.
ME: I don't get it.
ME: Oh, wait, do you mean "hey, girl"?
MOM: Yeah, that's what I said.

redefining funk

My Gchat status said "fuck Mondays!!!!!"

MOM: mei, why you said funk mondays

MOM: Mei, Are you on line?

ME: hello

MOM: Why you say Funk mondays?

ME: cuz I'm not happy about monday coming!

MOM: Is "funk" means sexy?

self-expression

"What a day! I am poop."

lumpia sauce

getting the phone-jeez

ME: Mom PICK UP THE PHONE JEEZ

MOM: what is a phone jeez?

last night at mcdonald's

MOM: Hi, I'll take the, uh . . . you know . . . the Big 'N'
Nasty!

MCDONALD'S EMPLOYEE: Um . . . we have a Big 'N'
Tasty?

going douche

After my parents got married and my mom had only been in
the United States about two years, they went to dinner with
my dad's coworker and his wife. The check came, and there
was talk of who would pay the bill. My mom had just recently
learned a new term and proudly announced . . .

"Let's all douche!"

mom, don't fret, it's goldman sachs

I left you message last night and don't know you got
or not. WE received message from Miss Nickle from
Goldensex(?) to ask part time job application response.
call home for any question.

more messy fries

My mom called me to ask what I want from In-N-Out
Burger . . .

ME: Can you get me the animal-style fries?
(30 minutes later, after she came home)
MOM: I asked for the doggy-style fries, but I think they
           ran out because they just started laughing.

special ingredients

MOM: I make special soup for you. It has special ingredi-
           ent. Guess.
ME: Um, I don't know. Ham?

MOM: It is not ordinary ham! It is prostitute.

ME: What are you talking about?

MOM: Prosti . . . prostituto!

ME: You mean prosciutto?

pick the weeds, too

Today i want you go home and do grass.

She meant "mow the lawn."

a lifelong spelling error

"My parents' intent was to name me Stephanie."

—STAPHANIE TUNG

dirty talk

My mother and I went to dinner. Upon leaving the restaurant, we noticed a cute little tabby cat lying on the dashboard on the inside of a car.

ME: Oh! Look at this cute little kitty in the car!

MOM: I wonder if they know he's in the car?

MOM: Go back inside the restaurant and ask if anyone left their pussy in the car!!!!

(after fits of laughter, I get in the car)

MOM: No! Seriously . . .

(a couple walks by our car)

MOM: Maybe it's their car!

(my mom rolls down our car window and points at the kitty-harboring car)

MOM: HEY! Is that your car? Your pussy is out in the car!

scoring with the chicks

CAR DEALER (to my dad): You can get a lot of chicks with this car.

MOM: Why would he want a chicken?

seafood emotions

ME (after a long day of school): I feel like crap.

MOM: Really? I feel like shrimp.

so fresh

MOM: YOU A FISHERMAN IN COLLEGE NOW

ME: Freshman mom.

MOM: FRESHERMAN

domestic violence not allowed

My friend and I were talking about some guys we met while in the car with my mother . . .

FRIEND: The blond one was hitting on you.

MOM: He PUNCHED you!?

wrong medication

My parents had this conversation in front of the doctor . . .

MOM: Don't forget you need to ask for Viagra prescription!

DAD: Why?!

MOM: For your allergies!

DAD: Allegra!

retarded attendance record

I was having a stressful AP testing week, so I asked my mom if I could take Tuesday off from school to study for the two other AP exams I had that week. My mom agreed to let me do so until she suddenly thought of one minor detail I seemed to have missed . . .

MOM: Are you sure that's OK? Won't they mark you retarded?

ME: . . . No. I think you mean tardy, Mom.

dog meat

We were at the drive-thru at KFC . . .

KFC EMPLOYEE: What can I get you?

MOM: I want a eight-piece meal with biscuits and mashed potatoes.

KFC EMPLOYEE: Regular or crispy?

MOM: Half regular and half crispy. Can I get it all dog meat?

KFC EMPLOYEE: Um, excuse me?

MOM: I want half regular, half crispy. All dog.

KFC EMPLOYEE: Ma'am, we don't do dog here.

ME: Sorry. My mom meant dark.

shoot hard, shoot quickly

My mom's basketball team was losing, so she started yelling at the TV . . .

"JUST PENETRATE ALREADY!"

a freudian flight

MOM: Dear Mei, do you remember you take one airline
            call Vigina. . . . . ?

ME: yea

MOM: how to spell

ME: . . . virgin

Suffice to say, my mother had an unfortunate experience on Google.

black friday finds

> **MOM:** Look at new purse mom buy. Dubby dubby!
>
> **ME:**   Hah? Dubby Dubby?
>
> **MOM:** Yes. Isn't it beautiful?
>
> **(holds up her Dooney & Bourke handbag)**

gangbanging up

My girlfriend's mom was raised in Korea and is an ICU nurse in the States now. My girlfriend and her sister were giving their mom a hard time about something she had said . . .

> **MOM:** Why are you kids always gangbanging me?
>
> **MOM:** It is not nice, you always gangbanging me!

She meant ganging up on her. They burst out laughing and she just got more upset . . .

> **MOM:** You kids are bad, always gangbanging me!

the warmth in your heart

I received a personal introduction from someone. I want
to reply, can I say the following.

1. Thanks for your introduction, I can feel your warm
heart.

2. Thanks for your introduction, it's very warm.

Which one or other suggestion . . .

—Ma

paying for prostitution

I was at a college career fair and was in the middle of an engag-
ing conversation with the admissions officer of the school I
was MOST interested in . . .

MOM: Oh . . . I see . . . Well, will my daughter be about
to afford this prostitution?

(about a second later)

ME: INSTITUTION?!?

ADMISSIONS OFFICER: Well, yes, we have a lot of . . .
scholarships . . . though there ARE nice jobs on
campus you can take to support yourself.

mom likes a man in uniform

My family went to a plane show where there were people in the army next to jets and fun stuff like that. It was a particularly hot day and these army men were wearing their full suits. We were already looking at one of the jets when this exchange happened . . .

MOM: I feel so hot for you! It is very hot weather today!
SOLDIER: Uh, thanks . . .

What she really meant was "You must be hot in your uniform." And the soldier was pretty creeped out.

fee vs. free

My mom got a bill from Sam's Club and was strangely excited. I had never seen her so excited about a bill before, so out of curiosity I looked over and saw a late fee for almost $125.

ME: Mom! Why didn't you pay the bill!
MOM: Sam Clup give me the free money!
ME: No, you have to PAY or else that fee will get higher.

MOM: What? I thought the late free?

ME: No, FREE has an R, FEE means you have to pay.

MOM: Dang Sam Clup, try to trick the Asian people.

prostitution is the new profession

MOM: I don't feel like going to work today. I want to play hooker.

ME: You mean, HOOKY?!

seductive examinations

MOM: I do not want to colonoscopy. That's OK. The nurse said I will be seduced.

ME: You mean, SEDATED?!

MOM: Oh. Yeah.

should've gone for korean food instead

We were on our way to a restaurant where you have to order at the counter. I was on crutches so I told my mom I didn't want to have to go up so she should order for me. It got a little complicated . . .

ME: I want baked mostaccioli with marinara sauce.

MOM: No, I'm not ordering for you.

ME: Come on, I just want to sit.

MOM: No, you order. I'll mess it up and you'll get mad.

DAD: I'll do it. She wants marinara.

MOM: No, that's not what she wants. See he already got it wrong. You order.

ME: He got the sauce I want right. I want baked mostaccioli with marinara.

DAD: OK, you want baked . . . mozzarella cheese?

ME: No. Baked mostaccioli.

DAD: Masta chili? What's that? Baked masta chili?

MOM (interrupts): No! She doesn't want baked.

ME: Mom, that's the part he got right . . . I want baked MOSTACCIOLI.

DAD: Baked? Wait, how can they bake pasta?

ME: What? What do you mean how could they . . . NEVER MIND. I'll order.

MOM: Good!

(five minutes later)

MOM (to me with a smile): I'm going to eat all of yours. I don't know how to say it, but I know what it is.

ME: OH MY GOD!

easter dessert

MOM: Try this! It's an Italian Easter pie. My friend at
work gave me the recipe.

ME (takes a bite): Uhhh . . .

MOM: Can you guess the flavoring?!

ME: . . . It tastes like Fruity Pebbles.

MOM: Ta-da!

(holds up bag of Jolly Ranchers)

ME: What on earth?

MOM: The recipe called for "candied fruit," so I asked
Dad to pick some up, and he brought back these.

ME: . . .

MOM: He almost brought back Gummi bears, but I told
him no.

vintage is in

MOM: Ohhh, Bee, I like your sweater! Where did you get
it from?

ME: It's from Anthropologie.

MOM: Oh, wow!

(a few weeks later)

MOM: Bee, when are you going to get me a sweater like
          yours from Greek mythology?

oliver oil

evenlops and oddlops

an unintentional souvenir

ME: Did you buy anything from the swap meet today?

MOM: Yes, I got CD holder . . . and this hat.

ME: MOM! Do you know what's on that hat?!?!

MOM: Yes, it's a city in Mexico. The hat was on sale.

ME: MOM! The city is Tijuana, not Marijuana!

CHAPTER THREE

technological competency

Desperate to understand her American children, the quintessential Asian mom attempts to delve into her kids' lives by participating in the world we love most: the technological one. While most of them are still learning their way around the keyboard, the effort they exert simply to eject a DVD is absolutely adorable. Plus, a painstakingly typed-out text message is worth a thousand words—even if the punctuation is completely nonsensical. In spite of their best efforts, there's much to learn. Let's not even get started on the way our moms surreptitiously comment on our blogs using fake names . . . alongside their real emails. From video-chatting on Skype (better known as "Skypee") to learning Gmail etiquette, our moms are going above and beyond as they take the Internet by storm. With their recent debut on Facebook, their invasions of our privacy are reaching unprecedented levels. Why not give them more channels through which they can commentate on our lives, right? At the end of the day, our moms don't quite grasp the concept of YouTube just yet . . . and their WPM could use a little help from Mavis Beacon herself. But when every text, email, and chat message is accompanied by emoticons in waves and droves, somehow our frustration at their technological ineptitude just fades away.

youtube predators

My mother is very protective. After she watched a *60 Minutes* special on online predators, we had the following conversation while I was watching a video blog on YouTube . . .

MOM: Who is that guy?

ME: I don't know.

MOM: Why is he talking to you??

ME: It's a video.

MOM (at the computer): GO AWAY, MY DAUGHTER DON'T WANT TO MEET UP AND TALK TO YOU!

blaming the mouse

When the mouse refuses to be dragged through the mouse-pad. Whose false is it? Is the mouse wheel not spinning or the mousepad is worn out? Which should I replace?):

Mom

here, have two

MOM: get transcript

ME: ohkay, yeah I got it. Can we go get my shoelaces today? :)

MOM: Ok

ME: Mom, you're wasting my texts by just texting one word back! -_-

MOM: Bye bye

straight to the point

Hello son it is test I am learning easy way to sand text massage I love you

i spy

A friend posted a photo of me with particularly bad posture, so I commented, "You're lucky my mom can't see this!" Later, my mom was creeping through my little brother's Facebook and sent this message . . .

Subject: hunchback

i seen it. (mom)

personalized instruction manual

I was showing my mom how to use the DVD player and she took notes. I found the notecard that she wrote the instructions on some months later . . .

DVD PLAY

1. press on

2. press eject key

3. put disk

4. sit down

5. press play key with remote

6. watch

+text+msging+

ME:	Hi Mama, can you call me in the morning to make sure i'm awake? Love you.
MOM:	Did+u+turn+ur+hw+in+on+time+anak+
ME:	Yea. Do you know how to press the space button instead of the plus signs?
MOM:	No+bcos+even+though+i+press+space+button +i+still+see+plus+i+dont+kno+how+to+erase+ so+you+need+to+erase+the+extra+letters+ after+this+txt+msqp0o5rrfsb+ja7h
ME:	are you sure you know how to use text mama? press the other button, like if you are pressing pound, use the star, or try 0.
MOM:	I know how to text now period i still need to learn d language use in this period
ME:	Mom. . . . try pressing 1 for the signs.
MOM:	ok,.

email add

hi its mom.the door is in . Learned how to jack up a house, drill cement. Dad is still a buster. . . . I need a new cell phone. Need Peek email item for xmas. It's hard to find. Maybe you can get your apple laptop back from the porn shop. You can keep contacting the police in PA. It's fun being home with Dad. This is a test for Seniors. Maybe Delicious Orchard's has nickolost?

Bye
lov mom

a distaste for punctuation

Hey Jonathan:I still can not get into the computer and if you have a chance sent dell a e-mail and see they can sent you the dis and we can pay for it and get my computer going and pls get in to my gmail Odessa had send me the picture and she want your picture and your girls picture just use my gmail address

Mom

a lesson in emoticons

My mom was trying to figure out how to do the Asian emoti-
con face: -_-

MOM: _—_
ME: HAHAHAHHA
MOM: only can do that
MOM: this computer is no good why cannot

number-happy texting

MOM: how do i make happy face?
ME: I think on your phone you press 1 over and over
       again to get each symbol
MOM: IIIIIIIIIIIIIIIIIIIIIIIIIIIIIIIII

instant messaging 101

MOM: woolalasoo i am cool
ME: Yes you are, haha
MOM: i am your cool mom

ME: The coolest mom in the whole world <3

MOM: <3

<3

>3

<3

:)

ME: Haha! You learned how to make hearts!

MOM: :P :) :P

ME: . . . And faces apparently :P

MOM: ^-^

^_^

:D

ME: Rofl hmm..

MOM: >:O

;) :(

:O

:o

>:o

<3

ME: <3 Haha. Okay I have to go. Talk to you later
         mom.

MOM: Byebye!

when asian moms yell

MOM: Dear, IS EVERTYINH OK?

ME: yup

MOM: THEN WHY YOU DON'T SLEEP?

ME: just got my internet to work :D

MOM: DON'T SLEEP TOO LATE IT IS NOT GOOD FOR YOUR HEALTH

ME: ok

ME: why are you talking in caps

MOM: oh

electronic explosives

MOM: I just heard on news that cell phone can blow up! Don't use the cell phone too much!

ME: You just called me on my cell.

MOM: Oh! OK, I hang up now!

1337 h4×0r programmer mom

A few days after my little brother and I explained the notion of 1337 to my (very, very computer literate) mom, I received a couple texts from her after she dropped me off at school.

> **MOM:**   Lunching. Then leaving 4 home. do u n33d us 4 anything?
> **MOM:**   How u lik3 my l33t

better than farmville

My mom loves her Facebook applications and checks them every day. She left this note on my dresser . . .

Alanna, if I'm not home at 5' O Clock p.m. please check my Cafe World and click my cook food okay. I love you. Thanks!

experiments in texting

MOM: Thisisyourmom.Iamtextingyou.

MOM: I.Dont.Know.How.To.Space.The.Letters.How?

MOM: Diditwork?

MOM: Howaboutnow?Isitworking?

MOM: Ididthat.

MOM: Ok.I.Am.Calling.Jed.He.Has.The.Same.Phone.

MOM: As you can see now I know how to do!

MOM: Listen to my new message! I wont answer. Call now.

New voicemail message:

Hi. This is your mom. Or your friend. If you do not fit into one of these categories, please do not call me. Thank you.

perseverance in texting

My mom had just learned to text the day before . . .

> Dear d Sure i wil meet you at time 7p square soon no
> 7p it is a tzphgg typing earror soppps Oh i give up

hi hi hi

I got this text from my mom after tennis practice . . .

> Hi emily i just want to hi to you Hi and hope your team
> will score love mommy do you

away message speak

My mom always asks me to help her with her English, especially when it comes to her grammar and vocabulary. One evening while I was still at work, I saw my mom on Yahoo! chat and decided to say hi. With no immediate reply, I left my desk to attend to something else. This is what I saw when I returned 15 minutes later . . .

> **ME:**   hi mom
> **ME:**   are you there?
> **MOM:**   mei
> **ME (autoreply sent to "MOM"):** I am currently idle.

MOM: you

MOM: you just testing my english, when i look the word
             "idel" i don't understand what that mean. i have
             to check dictionary right away, now i know waht
             meaning

MOM: that mean "nothing to do?" you have time?

MOM: no answer?! okay byebye!

MOM (autoreply): "MOM" signed off.

internet proficiency

ME: What browser are you using?

MOM: Google.

ME: Google is not a browser. Are you using Internet
             Explorer?

MOM: Yes, I'm using the Internet.

ME: . . .

spring is the season

My mom forwards all chain mail, jokes, warnings, and mis-
cellaneous email spam she gets onto all her loved ones. I still
get thrown off by the occasional email that makes me wonder

how much she understands of what she's sending along. Why would you forward the below joke to the rest of your family?! (No, we definitely don't have that kind of relationship.)

> **Subject:** Easter joke—not the best, but cute
>
> I know what you're thinking but it's funny.. . . .
>> What did the Easter egg say to the boiling water?
>> "Its gonna take a while to get me hard, I just got laid
> by some chick."

hi! this is only a testing

My boyfriend bought his mom a laptop for her birthday. I had given her some "computer lessons" in the past so she emails me frequently to make sure she's doing tasks properly. She recently figured out how to use Gchat and messaged me at 1:30 a.m. . . .

> **BOYFRIEND'S MOM:** L, again, this is only a testing. if
>   you receive, let me know.
> **ME:**   yep. i got it.
> **BOYFRIEND'S MOM:** what time do you usually go to bed?

ME: usually at midnight or 1.. right now im trying ot finish studying for my exam

BOYFRIEND'S MOM: OH! I do not know you still have exam! When's your next exam?

ME: at 9am

BOYFRIEND'S MOM: Just now I forgot to press enter. That's why it took so long for you to receive. Anyway, when you said 9am, do you mean tomorrow morning?

ME: in 7.5 hours

BOYFRIEND'S MOM: OK! Do not study too hard! BYE!

dygi? (don't you get it?)

My mom was talking to my sister about a recent relationship snafu while my dad, my other sister, and I listened . . .

MOM: So you had LQ?

US: What?

MOM: Love quarrel . . . duh!

(later)

MOM: So, it was an MU?

US: A who?!

MOM: Mutual understanding!!

fruit-feeding through skype

CHAPTER FOUR

brutal honesty

It's a miracle we emerged from adolescence with even the tini-est bit of self-worth intact—pressure from mainstream media to live up to unrealistic beauty standards is almost laugh-able when compared to the lifelong body criticism of a ruth-less Asian mother. We're hard-pressed to remember a return home from college that wasn't accompanied by a barrage of comments from family friends about our increasingly large size and shape. Our own moms' favorite adjective to describe our female bodies can roughly be translated as "hefty"—a term that epitomizes the Chinese inclination toward passive-aggressive insults. While the comments our parents make might come off as borderline offensive or downright rude to outsiders, growing up in a compliment-deflecting culture means we've grown some very, very thick skins. Where non-Asian friends are still scratching their heads as to how we unflinchingly accept the ego abuse on a day-to-day basis—well into adulthood—it's just another thing we've come to expect. At the end of the day, we're grateful to our mothers for their tough love. From years of downplaying our accomplishments to pinching our muffin tops in public, their well-intentioned criticisms have desensitized us to the cruelest insult and humbled us low to the ground. And on the bright side, any compliment they do let slip is more gratifying than a 4.0 GPA or a couple of pounds lost. Like they say: Honesty is the best policy . . . right?

the things we lack

My mom was sick, and I went to her room to bring her some tea. (Backstory: I have a jewelry line on the side.) In her bedridden delirium, the first thing she said to me . . .

"How come you have no boob? You need to make a lot of jewelry and get boob job."

true love

After my second pregnancy, I had this conversation with my mother . . .

> **MOM:** Waaaaa! You got so fat! You look like a fat person swallow your face!
>
> **ME:** That's really nice, Mom. I love you, too.
>
> **MOM:** I love you that is why I tell you. Only mother who love their child very much would tell them they are ugly. If I hate you, I would tell you, you are beautiful and you should eat more food. Eat more chocolate. Person who tells you eat more, they the one that hate you! Not me, I love you so much so I put you on diet, help you keep your husband.
>
> **ME:** There is nothing wrong with our relationship . . .
>
> **MOM:** For now! But stay too fat too long and he gonna look for pretty skinny girl and what happen to you? Fat, ugly with babies and no man. Poor you!
>
> **ME:** Don't worry!
>
> **MOM:** Don't worry? How can I not worry? I only one worry for you! Did he take life insurance out on you?

ME: MOM!!!!!
MOM: I just worry, that's all!

suicide watch

MOM: hey
ME (autoreply): drowning myself in the hudson river. Ugh,
        school.
MOM: Just go to the passaic river. Nearer

a compliment-worthy haircut

From: Me

I cut my hair! Here's a picture just in case you don't
recognize me when you see me.

From: Mom

Marning Hui Hui, We saw your hair cut pictures, did you
gain the weight? See you Saturday !!!

Baba, Mama

lifelong dissatisfaction

ME (showing her my new car): See, Mom? This is it!

MOM: Oh, look good! No more *dong cha**!

ME: And I just got that job, too! NOW are you happy?

MOM: Yes, I'm happy.

ME: NICE!

MOM: Now make me grandson and white you teeth.

very, very fat arm and leg

I saw some pictures that is we took from Bao-Bao's wedding party. You looks very, very fat especial your arm and leg. I will e-mail you when I figual out how to e-mail you. I know you don't like to hear that but I think you really need to do weigh watch out and stop to eat any sweet foods. When you age go up that will be very difficult to do diet. Trust me. I am you mother I always tell you truth. You need do some excise expecial for your arm and leg.

Love

Mom

---

* Korean for busted ride.

a wall décor critique

MOM: Hey, why you have all the black guy on your wall? Your wall all cover in the black guy.

ME: They're different musicians I like.

MOM: No. You look like the gay. You invite girls here, they going to think you the gay. You so skinny already, OK? Don't go look like the gay guy.

a fear of tattooed hippies

Nwe, good to hear from you again and know that you finally finish your school term and are having lots of FUN. NO TATTOO PLEASE OR i WILL NEVER FORGIVE YOU. I sent you an e-mail to ask where you will be staying and you did not answer me. You said you are going to stay with friends. Who are these people? You also experienced all kinds of clubs and I am sure they are adult clubs. I don't want you to be too wide living like hippie and behaving like one with tattoos over your body.

In the mean time, stay cool and keep in touch.

Love, Mom

evil laughter

After being a secretary and financial adviser for years, my mother made the decision to start teaching . . .

> **ME:** i hope you can handle them
>
> **ME:** some kids are really crazy
>
> **ME:** i don't think i can ever teach
>
> **ME:** it'll drive me crazy
>
> **MOM:** if i get prove maybe i can get the certificate of teaching chinese
>
> **MOM:** anyway when i as ur age
>
> **MOM:** i will have same thought as u
>
> **MOM:** but till now after i got 4 kids like you guys
>
> **MOM:** i believe i can handle any kid
>
> **MOM:** ha ha ha . . . .
>
> **ME:** . . .

son, don't be lesbian

I'm a guy, and my mother gave me a talk about not turning out gay . . .

MOM: It's good that your friend Milcah is a lesbian.

ME: Yeah, I know.

MOM: Just don't be like her.

ME: What?

MOM: You know, the same way like her. Don't be that way.

ME: What are you talking about?

MOM: You know, she is a girl and she like other girls. I just worry you gonna be turn like her.

ME: You don't want me to like girls?

MOM: No, I don't want you to be lesbian.

an unappetizing complexion

I went to dinner with my mom as soon as I got off the plane. My mom was sitting on my right and saw the acne on my cheek. She shook her head and sighed.

ME: What is it, Ma?

MOM: After seeing your face, I don't have appetite no more.

From that day on, I wore makeup every day before seeing her!

humans are clean shaven

I decided to grow a beard. My mom saw me on Skype a few weeks later . . .

> **MOM:** You need to shave.
>
> **ME:** I'm trying to grow them out.
>
> **MOM:** No, don't do this to me. Shave them off.
>
> **ME:** I think it'll look good.
>
> **MOM:** You should look like a human.

connect the dots

I visited my parents after nearly a year of being away and was talking to my mom about how I was doing at my new job . . .

> **ME:** So, it's really busy, but they said I've been doing really well, and I've been doing a lot of volunteer stuff, which is good for promo—
>
> **MOM (cutting me off out of nowhere):** Your face have so many dot dot dot. Dot dot dot all over. You eat too many junk thing?!

(the next day, at a Chinese restaurant my mom's friend works at)

MOM'S FRIEND (in Cantonese): Oh, your daughter is so pretty! Pretty girl!

MOM: What?! No, look at her face!

CHAPTER FIVE

mama's train of thought

Years of being their offspring mean we've caught on to most of the ways in which our mothers' minds work. We can antici-pate their unnecessary—and most likely unhelpful—driving tips or predict the conversation that will occur the day after they meet our prom date. ("What race is he? What colleges did he get into? What do his parents do?" We're not *getting married*, Mom.) But right when we start to think nothing our moms could say or do would surprise us ever again, their logic will take them to the most absurd of conclusions. Sometimes, we even find ourselves scolding them for the occasional inad-vertently offensive statement that comes out of left field. The rest of the time? We find ourselves scratching our heads in complete bafflement—while doubled over in laughter.

Here are tried and true methods for giving your Asian mother a heart attack:

- Bring home a non-Asian guy and introduce him as your boyfriend.

- Get a tan.

- Buy her a present that brings misfortune according to age-old Asian superstitions.

- Show her a B+ math test.

- Go up a jean size.

- Announce your homosexuality.

cause and effect

There is a hate crime happened this week in New York suburban. 7 teenage boys beat a latino in his 20s to death.

Be careful. I don't know if this is because we elected a black president.

Love, mom

rape prevention tactics

Be sure to wear lots of underwear, so if you get rape it'll take them longer and you can escape.

dirty hands

MOM: Why do people punch each other's hands now?

ME: What are you talking about?

MOM: Did you see those guys on TV now? Instead of a handshake they punched each other's knuckles.

ME: Oh, that. No, it's just the "cooler" way of a handshake now, Mom.

MOM: I thought it's because they thought the hands are dirty!

gay and youthful

After getting a satisfactory haircut from an Asian hairdresser . . .

ME: I think that hairdresser was gay.

MOM: Really? Poor him . . .

ME: Hm?

MOM: So young, and already gay!

in possession of uterus

I am a 28-year-old single woman. I walk into the kitchen Christmas morning in sweats but no socks . . .

MOM: Ai-goo! Why you not wear socks?

ME (looks around, as it is 60 degrees out): It's not cold. (I point to my father's similarly bare feet) And Daddy doesn't have socks on.

MOM (indignant): It different with Daddy. Daddy doesn't have uterus.

black is the new black

While looking at pictures of some Asian girls . . .

YOUNGER SISTER: Is that Tiffany?

OLDER SISTER: Wow, she got really dark!

YOUNGER SISTER: She must've gone on vacation or some- thing. She's really tan.

MOM: Dark cool now. Obama black!

deep-clean pre-clean

ME: What are you doing?

MOM: Cleaning the house.

ME: Isn't the house cleaner coming tomorrow?

MOM: Yeah, but we can't have it messy!

white people steal underwear

another news for you our backyard neighbor finally sold
their house and move out there yesterday, i'm happy,
there will be a young couple move in , they are asian?
i will hang my cloth line out again.

mom

yummy little cracker

I'm Taiwanese-Chinese and my wife is Caucasian. Our son,
David, was the first grandchild on both sides of the family. Naturally, my Taiwanese mother got excited and bought
him a million articles of clothing, including a T-shirt with a

picture of a rocket and the words "Little Firecracker" on the front. The subsequent conversation went like this . . .

MOM: Why do they call a child who wears this shirt a firecracker?

ME: I don't know . . . Probably because firecrackers are small but loud and colorful, just like kids?

MOM: Hmmm. Makes sense. (stroking David's hair lovingly) My little cracker . . .

ME: . . . (cracks up)

MOM: What?

ME: Uh, Mom, "cracker" is a derogatory term that non-white people call white people. Not so good, when David is half white.

MOM: Why call a white person "cracker" to insult them?

ME: I don't know. Maybe someone thought white people are bland and boring like a saltine cracker.

MOM: But crackers are delicious!

ME: Yes, they're good with soup, but this has nothing to do with David's shirt.

MOM: I do not understand insulting someone by calling them a tasty food. I eat crackers all the time!

ME: Mom, this conversation has gone on, like, five min-
          utes too long.

(silence)

MOM: Well, I still like crackers.

cultural clashing

ME: So Nini has a new boyfriend.

MOM: Oooooh? What is he?

ME: Um, Vietnamese . . .

MOM: Oh! That good, very good.

ME: And Mexican.

MOM: So he a tamale eggroll.

behind bars

where are you now, i have been email you for 3 days,
and there is no response, and I am in dad's store now,
dad needs to go to lunch with popo and his families,
     you make me so worry, i even think you were caught
by police and put in jail, because you are so crazy,

i even call jessica's mom, and she is in Taiwan now,
she can answer her phone.

are you in your room? or did you go soemwhere Fri,
and Sat?

mom

gay profile pic

My mom sent me this Facebook message regarding a photo of
me kissing my roommate on the cheek . . .

Jean,

Your picture shows you are gay that is no good.

Mon

midlife growth spurt

MOM: Keep play basketball. You will grow taller!

ME: I'm 29 years old. I think I've stopped growing by now.

MOM: No, you can growing! Everyone growing all the time!

ME: . . .

MOM: Also, keep jumping!

just don't trust boys

Earlier today, my dad sent me an email saying that he wanted to get my mom an iPhone for Valentine's Day.

> **ME (not wanting to give anything away):** Hey, Mom . . . what would you do if someone just comes up to you and asks you if you want an already paid iPhone?
>
> **MOM:** Don't trust commercials on Internet. They steal money from you and give you a lot of bad emails.
>
> **ME:** No. Um . . . my "friend" just asked me if I would accept an already paid iPhone. I said yes. But, if you were in my shoes, what would you say?
>
> **MOM (disregards question completely):** Was it a boy?!?!?
>
> **ME:** No! It was . . . never mind.
>
> **(silence)**
>
> **MOM:** If it was boy, say no.

anti-smoking campaign

My mom is always suspicious. She always automatically concludes that I must be smoking and tries incredibly hard to bust me for smoking. (I don't smoke.)

SCENARIO A

MOM: Are you hungry?

ME: No, Mom.

MOM: Why aren't you? It's way past dinnertime . . . You're smoking, aren't you? Smoking leads to lost appetite.

SCENARIO B

MOM: What are you doing?

ME: I'm doing laundry.

MOM: Why? You never do laundry! You're hiding something . . . You must be smoking. You're smoking, aren't you?

ME: Mom . . . I just wanted to be helpful. Forget it. You can do the laundry for me.

SCENARIO C

MOM: Did you just take another shower?

ME: Yes . . .

MOM: Why? That's the second time you took a shower!

ME: Mom, I just got done playing football outside. Chill out!

MOM: You're smoking, aren't you?

SCENARIO D

MOM: You look funny. Your face lost some weight.

ME: What . . . ?

MOM: You're SMOKING, aren't YOU!?

letter opener

MOM: Richard! You got a Christmas card! It's from a girl! I will read it to you!

ME: No, it's OK. I will open it when I get home next time.

MOM: No, it's OK. I already read it! Here. **(she reads slowly, having trouble with some words)** Oh, wow, so I looked up this word—"awesome"—it means "extremely impressive"! And she even says, "sunshine and rainbow!" Wow, she is totally into you.

ME: . . . Um, Mom, you don't have to open my mail, OK?

MOM: It's OK. I really don't mind. Have you eaten?

beware of pickpockets

For my first trip to Korea, my family's homeland, my mother very neatly sewed a Ziploc bag filled with $300 to the crotch of my favorite pair of underwear. When I protested, she said to me . . .

"Li-bah-kah! Never trust Korean people!"

Then she showed me how to hand wash them every night with Ivory soap so that the money wouldn't get wet.

homeless robots

MOM: Hey, when are you having kids?

ME: What? Why?

MOM: You need to have a plan! When a machine gets too old they don't bear good fruit.

ME: Mom, machines don't bear fruit.

MOM: And make sure you have smart kids. If they're dumb, I'll put them in recycling bin.

ME: . . . What are they going to recycle as?

MOM: I don't know. Homeless.

sit when you pee

My male friend went to the bathroom at my house, closed the door, unzipped his pants, and started doing his business. My mom walked up to the door and started listening in.

MOM: Eben. Eben. Are you standing up and peeing?

EBEN: No, Mrs. Wong.

MOM: Hey, I can hear you, OK? You stand up and peeing. I write sign above the toilet and say don't stand up to pee. Sit down, OK? When you pee standing up, it splash all over the place. So gross.

EBEN: OK, Mrs. Wong.

MOM: . . . I can't hear anything anymore. You sitting down or you done peeing?

parental guidance recommended

dearest daughter,

thanks for help! could you do some reserch make sure
those books good for your brother's age, please do not
relate to drug, sex, violence, horror, and gay those topic.

love,
mom

disco party with yo momma

ME: Do you want to leave Seattle at 7:30 or 8:30? 8:30
is more expensive.

MOM: OK, 7:30. How about come back? I hope to see
Seattle at night.

ME: OK. We leave Victoria at 7:00 p.m. and get to Seattle at 9:45 p.m. Is that OK?

MOM: If 9:45 the light still on?

ME: Umm, 9:45 is not dark yet in Seattle. It gets dark at
10 or later . . .

MOM: We can go to night club?

gary danko is a dirty robber

I received a desperate voicemail from my mom . . .

> I check mail and see bank statement . . . someone stole your
> $200!!!! Call bank!!!!! He put name as Gary Danko.

I called her back . . .

> Mom . . . Gary Danko is a restaurant in San Francisco . . .

in need of a tetanus shot

> ok son, I stepped on some metal wire attached to a snow-
> boarding ticket u left on stair. Hope I don't need a teg-
> nis(?) shot, that wire was pretty thick like a nail . . . ouch!

in case you were going to call

> I hope you didnot caught the cold. I finished the work
> and taking a nap now. Donot call me now, thanks.
> Mom

economy? environment?

Dear family

Our country is in deepest recession, people are loosing jobs, stock market is diving. We should go "Green" this Christmas. A general guideline should be the gift should be limited to under $20(one item exception for award good student with excellent school works).

Love
Mom

the orientation of ceilings

My mom wrote me an email describing how my six-year-old nephew had redecorated his room in some computer game theme.

Kind of worry when Mark picked a pink ceiling for his room! He changed it to a star sky ceiling. Relief!

trance is for potheads

That trance music is like . . .

"Ch-ch-ch-ch-ch—that's for people who smoke pot, you know?"

yakuza

My mom told me what my *jichan* (grandpa) thought of my tattoo . . .

you are made to so pretty and beautiful, the tatoo ruin
your value. that's what jicchan think
    and only yakuza* get tatoo

what's the equivalent of a benz dealership?

MOM: Where are you going?

ME: Oh, I'm going to meet up with friends in Hollywood.

MOM: You're not going to a bar, are you?

Yakuza is the Japanese mafia.

ME: Um, bye, Mom. I'm late now. Gotta go.

MOM: Remember you can't sell your car at a bar! Bars are for bad people. You'll only get bad people buying. You should always go to right market . . . *Never* sell your car in a junkyard!

types of crazies

I moved to New York from California, where my sister still lives with my parents. She's a nurse who works nights and goes out on her days off. This is the ending of an email my mom sent to me regarding my sister's lifestyle. Little does my mother know, the crazies in California don't have anything on the New York crazies . . .

Thanks anak. Have a nice and safe weekend. As an older sister, please tell your little sister to listen to us and not be going out and staying till 3 am on her days off. We are very concern about her staying out so late and coming home early in the morning with all the drunks, rapist, serial killers and crazy people out here. Hopefully she would listen to you.

Love you very much,
Mama

commuting is no joke in china

My mother-in-law wrote this in regards to our trip to China . . .

> There is only 1 fast (express) train to Nantung per night,
> I'm not sure we will be able to get 3 tickets in the same
> cabin if we can't buy the tickets early enough. Still I need
> those info ASAP. I assume the latest to buy is the night
> that I arrive to Beijing about 10 pm, don't forget there
> are 1.3 billion people in China.
>
> Mom

the symptoms, the symptoms!

Before I was supposed to go on a date . . .

MOM: Come get some dinner!
ME: I'm not that hungry. I don't really feel like eating.
MOM: WHAT?
MOM: . . . Are you pregnant with child?

homemade strawberry containers

My dad bought too many strawberries from Costco for my mom, so my mom insisted on giving me some. So that the strawberries would not get crushed in the three-minute car ride from their home to mine, my mom found the perfect way to transport them.

no trespassing, no violence

CHAPTER SIX

the love doctor

They might be in America now, but traditional Asian values die hard—especially when it comes to dating. Sure, arranged marriages might be out the window (much to our parents' chagrin), but that doesn't mean love is a free-for-all game. The rules are simple: No dating non-Asians. Don't be gay. Marry rich. Protect your carnal treasures.

Sometimes the attempts at finding their kids' future spouses are subtle—but most of the time, not so much. Either way, though, our moms are unapologetically up-front in their attempts at tinkering with our dating lives.

**ACCEPTABLE PROFESSIONS FOR
PROSPECTIVE HUSBANDS**

- Doctor

- Lawyer

- Neurosurgeon

- Optometrist

- Other highly lucrative careers involving med school degrees

- Computer science engineer

- Investment banker

- . . . Did we mention doctor?

going dental

The dentist is off for 2 weeks when you come back.
So no appointment. You can clean your teeth in your
school. Make an appointment in your dental school and
you may meet a dental boy.

Mom

hey, shorty

Also, please wear a high heel shoes, people said medical school do not like shorty student.

Take Care
MOM

how to produce boys

At the checkout counter of a Chinese grocery store, I over-heard this senior citizen–aged customer giving advice to the young mother working behind the counter . . .

"To get boy, eat lots of meat three months before action."

hot chested

I'm a married woman. My mom tried to give me advice on how to deal with my stuffy nose and congested chest . . .

ME: I have some Vicks VapoRub.

MOM: That is good! Ask Chad to rub the Vicks all over your
       back, and then all over your front. Make sure he rubs
       all over your chest until you get hot. Then go to bed.

faith and the burning question

Please!!! All the time prays with GOD . Love my
dougther Maryann you are my dream always.
    do you have boyfriend?

dropping a line

In an effort to get to know my brother's girlfriend, my mom
sent her this email . . .

Annie:

How are you
    I'm Andrew's Mom.
    Andrew said I can talk to you
    So I write this emai. my english is not good, Please
    don't laugh at me.

I just came back from Taiwan.

Is Andrew a good boy? Help me watch him!(joke)

anyway, very happy talk to you.

introducing soft-hearted men

Some guy might—might come visit your email. He's lawyer, and 4 yrs older than you.

and soft hearted/ that's all I know. I'm not sure if he'll visit your email or not. My church members now introducing all the single they know I think.. Sorry for the trouble. But as a Sa-mo-nim, I just can't say No to them.. pls, understand me.. I know this is not the right time to do that you have not much of time.. still I want you to have dinner dating sometime.

mom, with great love, and God Bless you . . .

give him space, space

hey, why you need some one to dance with??? you can dance by yourself. Remember, i told you men need SPACE. don't push too much. If he did not call, the only

way woman can do is "does not care" and when he
called, just pretend very cold, until he asked you. haha,
space, space. Also he might be very busy in the school.
Don't worry,he is just type of men, not too romatic, not
too considerate, just like daddy.

i miss you too.

mom with heart

slut scares

From: Me

Was freaking out as I haven't had my period since August
but I finally got it on Saturday so good news, you are not
going to be a grandmother ;)

From: Mom

WHA . . . a . . . a..T!! ..grandmother.??.. . . .to be pregnant
u would have to be sleeping with someone so are u being
a slut and sleeping around? Remember there is such a
thing as AIDS and it is worst than getting pregnant Pls
do not scare me . . . I hope u still have morales . . . leave

your preganancy to your other twin..and u can have the symptons in sympathy

Love
MUM

dinner party etiquette

In response to a photo I sent her of my boyfriend and me at a dinner party . . .

Dear Chougou,

Happy Birthday!!

I showed the pictures to grandparents which you sent to me last time , they were just laugh, they think you are still a little girl, Laolao said "??". Daddy always keep quite and no face expression.

The boyfriend thing is ok, just enjoy the period, but I have concern, you know. Remember what I said before, "marry the boy who has hold your hand", although era is different from mine, the core of life actually is same, you are smart girl, you know what should or should not do. I hope boyfriend could makes you both progress.

I guess daddy may anger if he saw wine instead of boy, alcohol can make trouble, you can not trust yourself if you drink alcohol. Just remember, if you drink in public, only one glass, and always hold the glass by yourself anytime. I am serious, remember what's mom said forever!!

Mommy always play annoying role, well, just do the best you can.

Love, mom

sister rivalry

From: Younger Sister
Subject: Fwd: good daughter
To: Me

jealous?

————Forwarded message————

From: Mom
Subject: good daughter
To: Younger Sister

As a daughter, you are a lot more dependable.

I will run by you first with the great husband prospects first.

places to meet men

ME: My boyfriend broke up with me.

MOM: What? You had a boyfriend? How old? Is he Chinese or Vietnamese? Did you meet him at a disco or casino? Don't meet boys at discos or casinos—they only want one thing.

6 a.m. voicemail

"Jiejie, you should get new boyfriend. The grandma want to see you get marry. Mommy didn't tell grandma about your old boyfriend the Japanese because grandma is very old and I am afraid you love Japanese make her heart sick and maybe then the grandma die. So Mommy did not tell him. Please find gentle boy and introduce to Mommy and Daddy. OK if Japanese. Just remember to don't tell the grandma. She is very old. Love you! Don't call back if you are too busy, Jiejie. Study hard! Bye bye."

matchmaker mom

MOM: So, how Alex doing? Do he have girlfriend yet?

SISTER: No, Mom. Alex is gay. He's been outwardly gay since high school. That was eight years ago.

MOM: Ohhh . . . so, why he never have girlfriend?

SISTER: Because he's gay, Mom. He likes boys.

MOM: Why do he choose that?

SISTER: Mom, he didn't choose that. He's just gay.

MOM: Ohhh . . . let me know if Alex want me introduce to someone. I can introduce to nice girl.

the nonconfrontational sex talk

MOM: You might meet a boy, and when you shake his hand, you feel electricity!

ME: What?

MOM: Feeling electricity is good, but make sure you don't feel electricity when you shake every boy's hand.

latin-american lover

I'm so happy that you finally got the chemistry going with the right boy. Enjoy the ride, and let the future unveiled by itself. Latin American makes the best lover. I'm glad he is not the combination of . . . tall, handsome, and be the doctor. Flawless person is an insane!

on the positive side

MOM: Cha-lie-goo . . . I got your mail. It look important so I open.

ME: Um, OK, what is it?

MOM: It say gonorrhea . . . negative . . .

ME: Um, Mom?

MOM: Chlamydia . . . negative . . . HIV negative . . .

ME: MOM! Stop reading that!

MOM: Syphilis . . . negative. Everything look OK.

ME: Mom!

MOM: Cha-lie, be careful.

contraceptive witticisms

you still virgin? you know.. . . . . . . no balloon, no party
ok? Ok

animal attachment

Dear beloved Susan, I told Grandmother that you are
not happy, and depressed lately. This is strictly her opin-
ion; You are attached your lovely dog instead of your
lovely boy friend. This relationship is interfered by dog's
existence.

   She suggested that you should sell the dog to other
dog love person. You spend more attention to him to
have more precious relationship always. It will help your
personal relationship more closer. She really think Ryan
is sweet, caring, patient and talented good man, you
should respect and appreciate to take your meanness. At
the same time, you should control your mental unstable,
before you regret permanently.

   I hope you find healthy solution! I am sorry to deliver
unpleasant message, but Grandmother is old and she

knows things that we did not think of. She also said, living with dog for a long time, is not healthy for human. There are something about within their hairy body contains.

I love you darling!

Mom

rape warning

How are you? Do you have enough money ? My Camary was hit by a high school kid and it was totaled. Please watch your safety. I do not want anything happen to you. The boy who goes with you did he behave or respect you ? I am worry he will rape you.

I started my new job. It is so busy. Wish you can take good care about yourself. And behave. Please respect your body.

relationship consultant

After a recent breakup . . .

Dear Sue,

Focus on med school applications. Now is not time for socializing . . . yahoo dating tips:

http://dating.personals.yahoo.com/singles/ datingtips/68789/heartbreaker-101;_ylc=X3oDMTFpNm Y5bTIyBF9TAzI3MTYxNDkEc2VjA2ZwX3RvZGF5BHN sawNoZWFydGJyZWFrZXItMTAxBHp6A2Fi

Love,
Mom

on sax before marriage

Now I realize the difference between students graduated from Yale or Harvard and other regular university. So your dad and me are not worried about your job, but worry about one thing which your dad wants me to talk with you.

I understand you, like all other young people, would like to experience the love, a romantic love. We also know, to stop young people having sax before marriage is impossible, but we'd like to remind you, at least you should always protect yourself well.

1. Do not let pregnancy happen.

2. Prevent the disease. your skin is not good, I am afraid the first time having sex you might get pain and suffered.

with love,
Mom

kisses have cooties

I was telling my mom about a guy I was interested in . . .

MOM: so anything happen with him?
ME: we kissed
MOM: yuuuuuuuuuuuuuuuuu*
MOM: kissing is for husband only
ME: hahahaha
MOM: no sex before blood test though
MOM: that i'm more serious.

---

* Translation: ewwwww.

pda papparazi

In the school parking lot after class, my mom pointed out an Asian couple making out near the bathrooms . . .

MOM: Aiiiiiiiiiii-YAAAAAAAAAA! Can't they do that behind bushes or something? If you eveeeeeeeeeer get boyfriend, don't let me see do something like that!

ME: Don't worry. I wouldn't dare to.

MOM: Good. Because if you do, I take picture and send it to Grandma. And then when Grandma get heart attack, you pay hospital bills.

deflowering

This guy gave me a rose, and I put it in my room. My grandma saw it and told my mom . . .

MOM: Who gave you rose?

ME: What?

MOM: The rose in your room!

ME: Oh, just this boy . . .

MOM: What boy? Don't you know rose means sexing.

ME: Sexing?

MOM: Yeah, sexing. You know. Sexing.

ME: It's just a rose.

MOM: You be careful! He wanting to sexing you.

sour milk

My mom has been pressuring me to get married ever since I graduated from college. I'm 26 and not looking to get hitched anytime soon. She brings up marriage in every single conversation that we have, whether it's related or not. I was talking to her about my upcoming birthday . . .

ME: So, for my birthday . . . **(starting to tell her plans)**

MOM: You need to really get married this year . . .

ME: Mom, I'm only 26, and I don't want to get married right now. We've talked about this so many times!

MOM: Yeah, well, you should get married soon. You turning 27, have three years to find good man and get married.

ME: Um, why three years?!

MOM: Girls no pretty when they pass 30. No guy going to marry you when you expire.

saying the inevitable

How are you? we are very fine. how is you eyes allergy ?
hope you will get better with med or some good items.
dont they have high tech item for it and make any comfortable? i hard many people have a suffer . you should
be busy for moving prepare. one thing i would like to
tell you that men is not best part nor living together,
so, please do not pregnant. as your mother, it is so sad
to say this. but if you want to live with men, this top-
ics is inevitable. you should take care yourself, protect
yourself. even parents cant help anything for it. if you
get married with dave i will be very happy when you get
baby. you know everything. no mention anymore. we
love you . take care. Mom.

dating analogies

Never give anyone a free trial and take your product
home. They must pay full amount first. Because if they
get free trial, I know because I sell cosmetics for so many
years, they will always return product.

applicable proverbs

Don't be easy. Don't be like a cow. Chinese people say, if a boy gets the milk for free, he has no need to buy the cow.

gardening advice

MOM: So, do you have boyfriend yet?

ME: No, no. Not right now.

MOM: This good. You must protect your rose.

ME: . . . my rose?

MOM: All girls have rose. It no good to lose it early. Boys want to pick your rose, but you no let them. If every boy pick your rose, garden will be empty! Then what give your husband, then? No one will want to marry you. Then you end up with old man with bad teeth, like Mama here.

ok is not ok

> **MOM:** You know, if you have a boyfriend now, it's OK. You're old enough to meet nice boys.
>
> **SISTER:** Thanks, Mom, I know, and no, I don't have a boyfriend.
>
> **MOM:** Good. Because if you do, I'll kill you.

please use your hand

Dear Mihir Beta,

How are you doing? I am missing you. Keep healthy. Sleep well and eat well. Please call and talk for few minutes. You keep saying, "I got to go". That is hurting. I would like to know what you are doing or how studying is going on. Do your best. Donot do too many things. This is the age to work hard and make your life. You have to make some sacrifices on some pleasures.

Donot get entangled with any girl. I know you want to have physical relationship with a girl. Please use your hand. It is safest way. For your stars only girl can give you problem now. I know all your friends have girl friend and you feel bad. Remember you will have a great life ahead of you. Donot accept any girl even if she comes to you. Just wait. Character is the most important thing in life.

Happy Diwali!!!!! for Friday. Pray to Divine Cosmic Energy to give you strength of mind, body and spirit.

My Blessings and Love to You,
Mom

no happy endings

MOM: i see . . . very good. . . . are you in the company now?

ME: no im at home finishing lunch

MOM: any juicy story?

ME: haha one of the guys I met in singapore likes mE

MOM: he ever in shanghai?

ME: he says he wants to visit

MOM: he is a local?

ME: singaporian yes

MOM: well . . . i guess no happy ending, haha

when boyfriends become extraterrestrial

> **MOM (in Vietnamese):** What's the name of that boy who's
> half Japanese that you're seeing?
>
> **ME:**   Eliot.
>
> **MOM (repeats in English):** AAAALien. I call him E.T.

be a man, answer the question!

My mom was trying to hook up my brother with some girl in
Beijing. My brother likes Italian girls though, and he was in
Iraq and not exactly available to date—doubly not interested.
Here's her pleading email . . .

> Please let me know if you want made friends with Lily
> or not, if yes, I will give your e-mail address to her and
> tell her don't talk anything about both of your jobs. only
> personal questions, she might come US on this summer
> for her nursing school and she want find job and stay in
> US. she was top student in university so she doesn't have
> problem of English, she already saw your picture and
> want make friend with you.

I won't ask you about 1985 thing anymore, I know what was happen, I already stooped relationship with aunt Linda. I will never see her again. please answer my question I don't think it is so difficult?? I'm not push you merry her just start be friend first. be like a man and answer the question. okay!!

Margaret said you want Italian girl but you cannot have cheese, milk how you can live with Italian. they eat cheese all the time! and after be mother most Italian woman become very fat. think about!!

mom

chinese zodiac beliefs

My mother lives in Taiwan and calls me every two weeks. I figured it was about time to tell my mother I was dating, and if anything I should be old enough to date, so she should be OK with it. Here's the conversation we had . . .

ME: Hey, Mom, so I have a boyfriend now. Are you OK with that?

MOM: Well, I'm fine with it, but I'm disappointed. I think you are a little too young.

ME: But I'm 18, Mom. I'm turning 19 in a few months.

MOM: Eighteen is too young! Chinese people like their daughters to start dating at 20, not 18. You are just a baby. The point is that you shouldn't let your father know.

ME: Why not?

MOM: Because he is a rabbit, and rabbits do not like sudden changes in their lives. On that thought—don't tell your Auntie Irene, either. She is a rabbit, too.

ME: I think she would understand. She knows me pretty well.

MOM: Doesn't matter. She is a rabbit. She's not like me, a monkey.

is your husband a virgin?

"Is Johnathan a nun?"

CHAPTER SEVEN

food and health

Don't slouch. Eat your veggies. Stop staring at the computer screen all day. From the moment we came out of the womb, we've been bombarded with reminders about how to best optimize our lifestyles according to our mothers' interpretations of archaic Eastern health rituals, random newspaper clippings, and figments of their imagination. There may not be scientific evidence that leftover grains of rice cause pimples or that leaving the house with wet hair gives you headaches in your old age, but years of conditioning mean we've developed a slight paranoia of breaching ancient wisdom. Still, if our mothers tell us to go to bed early one more time—especially while we're working on a lab report as part of their grand plan for us to become doctors—we might just stay up simply in defiance. While we whine and wrinkle our noses now at their nagging suggestions, suffice to say, in 20 years we'll be making our kids ginseng goji tea, too.

10 ASIAN KITCHEN NECESSITIES

- Rice cooker

- Hot water boiler

- Giant cleaver that could pass as a murder weapon

- Sesame oil

- A lifetime supply of garlic

- Apron with obscene flower prints

- Imported tea leaves

- An offensively large jug of soy sauce

- Economy-sized bag of rice

- Unidentifiable roots and herbs

workout tips

Well, last time I forgot to tell you an exercise, it's called "9 point exercise" from 1 famous old Chinese doctor in China. The 9 points are: 2 heels, 2 calves, 2 highest points of the bum, 2 shoulder blades and the back of your head; stand against the wall and try to make the 9 points touched the wall, it's not easy, but it can help to correct posture and then cure the shoulder/back pain, doesn't matter how long you do it, just whenever you're free, do this 1 or 2 minutes, once you get used to this posture, I believe the way you walking or standing will be beautiful!!!

Okay, will take my lunch now.

Love,
Mom

anti-aging hair

I need to remind you to use your fingers as a comb to brush your hair once a while can reduce gray hair due to the improvement of head blood circulation.

Remember to take Vitamin & Calcium is also very important to keep your dark hair and good health condition. Take care of yourself.

Love,

Mom

spring acne growth

Yes, Fremont is lower than 60 degree at night. . . .

Be sure to sleep 9 hours, however, remember even if you miss one night's sleep, it will take many many days to recover, to regain the energy. Especially, the pimples won't remember that you are catching up the sleep later on. When I travel overseas and suffer from jetlag, the payoff later on is PIMPLES POPPING UP LIKE DAF-FODIES IN THE SPRING, and lowering immune system and malfunction of digestive problems. . . .

I understand it is unavoidable as a college student, just like it is inevitable as a frequent traveller struggling for time difference.

Cheers and hope you are here so I can prepare soup to replenish your immune system. . . .

Mom

inappropriate dinner conversation

SISTER: Did you want some fish?

ME: No thanks, I don't like this type of fish . . . it has the weird black gooey skin with it.

SISTER: Really? It's really good for you. It's codfish.

ME: Errr, no thanks . . .

MOM: WHAT? YOU DON'T LIKE BLACK COCK?

(my sister and I start laughing)

MOM: What's so funny? Nobody likes black cock?

squat for sanitation

Joyce,

Do I look that old? Do you still squad and pee in the public restroom? Keep your own sanitary.

Love,
Mom

in fear of toxins

Hi, Gina,

Daddy left this morning via Delta. he will arrive JFK and then to Korea after 1 PM.

I do not see any problem eating kalbi marinated in rice wine. You can eat anything except Coffee and a lot of wine or liquor . . . or marijuana, cocaine..or other toxic food.

I leave meat in water for few min, squeeze to get rid of blood, remove all the fat, boil in hot water to get rid of fat..and then put them in soup or kimchi jjige . . .

I hop you eat as much as you want (for baby, too) whatever you like.. OKEE?

Love you,
Mom

hydrate, don't constipate

Hi, sons, the best way for constipation:fiber and prune juice (3-4 table spoon or more/a day). try it, if you need.

One bottle you can drink it about more than one mouth.
Bon, drink oil is not good method. Mom

the temperature of your edibles

Dear Children:

Attached the medical report. I know these article in
Chinese you might not understand at all. The key thing
is "do not drink or eat the ice cold staff. Special for your
breakfast, When you wake up and your body, stomach
still does not warm up and function appropriate yet, and
you give the cold food, it will cause the stomach muscle
clamp. (Just like you get up from warm bed you jump in
swim pool your body can not stand it.)

Gradually fail function and hurt your health in silence.

Having a warm health breakfast is very important for
your health. Everybody seems knowing it but does not
do it, special for your young generation. If you do not
have good eating habit now then all kind health problems
will appear early than your age

Doctor grandpa, he worked very hard for his life but
he always ate right and enjoyed his food, slowly his pace
not rushed and scooped food into his mouth.

Hope you guys could change your eating habits. Eating on time with health food, avoid cold staff, slowly and enjoy your food enjoy your life.

Love you all, Mom

unconscious

My Gchat status said: "Food coma."

MOM: what do you mean by food coma?

Thirty seconds later, I received the following voicemail from her . . .

Eric, I saw that you had a food coma? Are you OK? Please call back to make sure that you are OK.

testy with nuts

MOM: what are you doing now? why you on'y talk to me?
MOM: hi, Dear are you on line?
ME: i was making a smoothie, didnt eat dinner yet

MOM: finished it already?

ME: i'm drinking it now

MOM: Is testy?

ME: it's pretty good

ME: tasty

ME: not testy

MOM: that's all, you need eat some food for ennergy

MOM: pur some nuts

ME: you can put nuts inside a blender?

MOM: I don't know maybe a litter

anti-zit bedtime

MOM: You need to go to bed early so you look nice
          and pretty and not have shits on your face!

ME: ???

health tips

Dear Alex,

Some info share with you.

   *Don't use Micwave(not often).

*Don't close Micwave (at least 6 feet away) when you use micwave.

*Don't take too many kind of Vitamins(you still youth, not necessary), because cause your kisneys has burdon, not good for your Kisneys.

I love you forever

Mom

fat hormones

Do you have lot of pimples now? When Mommy your age I not have pimples because I have no hormones because I very skinny. You eat cheese, so you have fat, so you have lots of hormones so lots of pimples.

well, if you have a good-looking nose

Your eyebrows and eyes are good so when you at that age you should doing very well, especially the year of the nose, actually, your whole look is very good, don't worry, you will be rich. ha . .. . and ge ge too, because both of you have a good looking nose. trust me.

Open up own business always have stress but you
have to try to relax, when your stomach hurts don't
drink any beer or wine, are you feeling all right?

Mama

beware the asian glow

hi amelia,

how are you? how is Scotland? tall us little bid.
    becarful dont drink beer you face go red like me.
    ha ha i like picture you send
    wemiss you much

loveyou mom

dear druggies, leave ma alone

My place smell like someone smoke weeds, the smoke
are so strong gave bad headache. I can not open window
or run AC . Very bad air condition.

easy on the eyes

Do not ware your contact lances for a long period of
time, you'll get cornia infection easily, this is a news
on TV now.

yeah, terrence, why not?

Terrence;are you still Cough,why not going see Doctor.
If you still Cough you Lung may has problem,has time
go see Doctor.

webmd mom

I called my mom and told her I had a headache. This is what
she sent me . . .

Hi Cindy,

You may have migraine, which often occurs in the
young ladies due to stress, hormone change, and other
factor. It is an extremely debilitating collection of

neurological symptoms that usually includes a severe recurring intense throbbing pain on one side of the head (although in 1/3 of migraine attacks, both sides are affected). Attacks last between 4 and 72 hours and are often accompanied by one or more of the following: visual disturbances, nausea, vomiting, dizziness, extreme sensitivity to sound, light, touch and smell, and tingling or numbness in the extremities or face. You can take regular pain killer pill, or exceed migraine countertop pill, no kill yourself please. If you come back home this weekend, I can make some good food for you, or we can make some foods and take them to you at the school during the weekend.

How is your school work?

Mom

cutting out the crapohydrates

I noticed my mom was losing weight and asked if she was doing anything in particular. She responded . . .

"I am on a low crap diet."

menstrual advice

Subject: when you have period, sprot drink + warm water

when you have period do not keeping on taking pain killer because it will hurt

your kindney in the long run. I heard a lady keep on taking Pain Killer when

she has period come and now she needs to wash her kindney and she is not 30 yet!

if you have headach or period please mix the sport drink with warm water

and the ratio is 1 to 1 or 1 to 2 and the result is much better than pain killer!

Loves
Mom

when body parts combine

I came over to my girlfriend's house one time and I had a stomachache. This is the conversation I had with her mother, who is a nurse . . .

GIRLFRIEND'S MOM: Do you want something to eat?

ME: No, I'm not hungry.

GIRLFRIEND'S MOM: Why not?

ME: I'm not feeling well. My stomach really hurts . . .

GIRLFRIEND'S MOM (deep in thought): Ohhh . . . It's
    probably you have problem with your intesticles.

loooooove you, too

I had to wake up early the next morning for a job interview.
My mom sent me this text . . .

> pls sleep soon. nobody like swallen face and jumble eyes.
> goooooooooodluck.
> love mom.

i will tell you when you're famous

Hi, Mark

Since I told you I had six sense , you will be very famous
in future. Anyting you say, think twice or more,then
delivery your though to someone. I will tell you someday

why I Mention it. EAT WELL & EXERCISE WELL TOO.
TAKE VITAMINE EVERYDAY.

Love,
Mom

i'm not flat

I was sitting at the dinner table eating a salad and drinking
a cold glass of water when my mom sat down next to me . . .

MOM: If you want your boobies to grow you need to eat
hot foods. You shouldn't be eating so much cold
foods.

ME: Mom!

MOM (laughs): Hey, I'm just telling you so you know what
to eat.

forget stds

I started dating someone when I moved home after college.
My mom wasn't accustomed to the idea of my dating . . .

MOM: Don't let him kiss you.

ME: OK, Mom.

MOM: If he kiss you, maybe he has gingivitis and give you gum disease!

how to air out dirty lungs

Since you guys catch a cold too often, I would like to give you some advice. Spend 5 mins a day to get rid of dirty air, cold from your lung. Doing the jumping exercise I teach you this winter break. You need to jump until you sweat. Change your clothes if your clothes are wet. Remember open your mouse when you jump.

Mom

shark alert

ME: Ma, I'm going to the beach to bodyboard.

MOM: What bitch you going to, hah?

ME: Huntington, Ma.

MOM: OK, you be careful. Don't get bit by a shark. You don't have health insurance.

one by one

How my mom eats popcorn so the grease doesn't touch her fingers . . .

CHAPTER EIGHT

political awareness and political incorrectness

"Politically incorrect" might not be in an Asian mother's vocabulary. Scratch that—based on the regularity of their outlandish statements, we're pretty certain they're not even vaguely familiar with the concept. Unabashed racism, outright homophobia, and jokes in poor taste are all part of our mothers' inadvertent comedic routines. From nicknaming a Middle Eastern boyfriend "The Terrorist" to calling the Mexican gardeners "amigos," it's lucky our moms have that whole "confused foreigner" facial expression going on, or they'd have more things to worry about needing protection from than UV rays.

But while they may not give a hoot about America's unspoken social rules, our liberal hearts are atingle with glee at their recent efforts at participation in American politics. We can't say that their rationales for supporting one cause or another are necessarily sound, but the fact that they made it to the polls this past election? Now that's change we can believe in.

vegetable humor

dearest bao,

i made eggplant parmesan today with 3 different kinds of cheese. it was really good. didi said that it tasted like lasagna! i don't know why i like to copy down those Italian recipes so much. maybe because i like cheese a lot. anyway, this is a really easy dish to make too so i will teach you.

when i went to the middle-eastern store to buy eggplants, i noticed something really funny. there are different kinds of eggplant: chinese, japanese, italian, indian, and american. and the american eggplants are the biggest and fattest among all the eggplants! HAHAHAHAAHA. just like their people!

have a good night bao and a good day tomorrow!

Mama

political leader mix-up

MOM: So, it looks like that Osama guy is doing a good job so far after he got elected.

ME: Mom, it's not Osama. It's Obama.

a bit of obaamaaarama

Subject: A new president for the new generation

To All My Children

Last night I stayed up to watch the result and went to bed around 4 am. I love the victory speech of Obama and I have tears in my eyes, I listened to it 3 times on CNN, and on 2 other channels too. We went to a neighbor to watch the result with them and came home about 1 o'clock. Dad went to bed about 2 o'clock 'cause he wants to wake up early this morning to go fishing. I stayed up until 4 am to watch the celebration and watch the reaction from several foreign countries. It feels good to see the whole world seems so happy with the new president, it is so funny to hear the chinese pronounce Obaamaaa very much in chinese way, in Australia, in

some countries in Europe it is just so incredible to witness this phenomenon.

Melissa, did you receive the Obama button I sent
you??

Becky, I love your email this morning!!! I called Mrs
Cook last night at 1 am to talk about this election. I was
so happy I could not go to bed. This morning I call her
again and we talk about the election again for a long
time.

Michael, tomorrow Thursday auntie Janet will come
here with her friend and stay for two weeks. I will call
you one day when the kids are not so busy to let them
say hello to her.

Love to you all, Mom.

democratic choices

From: Me

Mommy & Daddy—

I am gay and I want the right to marry when I grow up.
Vote NO on Prop 8.

From: Mom

Are you voting? It's too late, we voted this morning.
Daddy voted yes and I voted no. You can't be gay, that's
for guys to be called only

From: Me

Then what am I to be called? And yes, of course I am
voting.

From: Mom

I thought that the girls are lesbian and the guys are gay.
First time voter for you? Young voters are usually for
Democrates until they work hard and make good money.

living in america

ME: Ma, did you go vote?

MOM: Mamta, the lines were so long . . . there was no
           parking this morning so I left.

ME: Mom, you're an immigrant . . . you've been through
           tougher times than this. You came to America with

$25 and now you're giving up your right to vote because you can't wait in line??

MOM: That was so long ago . . . we came to America for an easier way of life.

go bama, go bama!

GO VOTE AND MKE SURE TO DO FOR ME AND [YOUR SISTER] .JUST IN THOUGHT .WILL YOU NE HOME OR UR PLACE SO WE CAN COMMUNICATE SORRY FOR YOUR PLUG THAT IT DOESNT WORK . DID YOU ORDER NEW ONE ? LOVE YOU
   GO BAMA GO BAMA .
   SORRY CAPS

new presidency, new residency

"Now we have a Black House instead of White House!"

denying the sign

I recently explained to my mom what "Yes on 8" meant since there are a lot of signs in our neighborhood. We also just had two gay weddings in the family. On Thursday, at our neighborhood meeting, a woman running for a Senate seat in our district asked if we wanted a "Yes on 8" sign for our lawn. I respectfully turned it down, but then my mom laughed and said loudly . . .

"We cannot take! Our family has the gay!"

closet replacement

ME: Not all feminine guys are gay.

MOM: No . . . They probably just haven't come out of the cabinet.

politically aware

ME: Mom, do you know who you're going to vote for yet?

MOM: I don't know yet. I don't really know anything about
Obama Baracka.

ME: Obviously. You don't even know his name.

pokémon for president

ME: Mom, so you know Barack Obama, he—

MOM: Huh?

ME: Obama. Barack Obama?

MOM: Oh, you mean the Pokémon?

ME: No! The guy running for president!

our friends, the amigos

MOM: I driving around now and there so many amigos in
L.A.

ME: "Amigos," Mom? What are "amigos"? Do you mean
Hispanics?

MOM: Yeah, amigos.

ME: Mom, they are called Hispanics.

MOM: What? They amigos.

ME: No, Mom. They are Hispanics. Amigos means
"friends" in Spanish.

MOM: Yeah, amigos, friends. What's wrong with that?

ME: I don't think that's politically correct, Mom.

MOM: So what? They want to be amigos. That's what we
        call them in Taiwan.

lesbians of the middle east

I went with my family to a buffet where I had a dodgy oyster
and ended up hurling in the bathroom. The restaurant's manager came out to talk and apologize to my parents when I was
in the bathroom. When I came out, the most epic conversation with my mom ensued . . .

MOM: Oh, the manager came to talk to us. He said he
        was lesbian.

ME: Huh? You mean gay, right? He's male . . .

MOM: No, no, lesbian. He said he was from the Middle
        East.

ME: OHHHH!! You mean he's LEBANESE.

MOM: Yeah! Lesbian!

preventing 7-11

My mom was watching the news that a terrorist was stopped by passengers on a plane during Christmas and sent me this email . . .

> **We almost had another 7-11 this Christmas; thank god the terrorist was stopped!**

like . . . a tax return?

I called the Maternal Unit on Chinese New Year since it is customary to do so. This conversation occurred on the phone around 11 p.m. on January 26 . . .

ME: Hi, Mom.

MOM: Hi, Happy Chinese New Year.

ME: Thanks—you, too.

MOM: Thank you. You know, I want red envelopes.

ME: Um, who's going to give them to you?

MOM: Obama.

ME: Um . . . why would he do that?

MOM: Because it's Chinese New Year.

ME: Mom, he's not even Asian.

MOM: President Ma Ying-Jeou [of Taiwan] gave them out.

ME: That's because he's in Taiwan!

MOM: Do you think we have to ask Obama for them, or will he just hand them out?

ME: . . .

CHAPTER NINE

pop culture

There's nothing quite like sitting in the car with a friend when your mother begins to demonstrate her appreciation for Top 40 music by butchering rap lyrics in a most mortifying fashion. We have to give them credit just for trying—it's not easy to keep up with the Kardashians, after all, especially when they grew up in a completely opposite culture that pays zero homage to spray tans or enormous boobs. Like everything else in our relationships with our moms, when it comes to popular culture, sometimes we just have to meet them halfway.

MOM'S FAVORITE POP CULTURE ICONS

- Parrot Houston (Paris Hilton)

- Many More (Mandy Moore)

- Larry Porrey (Harry Potter)

- Papaya the Salesman (Popeye the Sailor)

- Bronze Pierce (Pierce Brosnan)

- Goldie Whoopberg (Whoopi Goldberg)

- PeeDiddilly (P. Diddy)

- Joe Low (J.Lo)

fatboy slim goes to china

We were in the car listening to the radio and the song "The Rockafeller Skank" by Fatboy Slim came on . . .

MOM: Is an Asian person singing this?

ME: I don't think so. Why?

MOM: Because of the chorus. "Right about now, feng shui brothers. Check it out now, feng shui brothers."

texan bird heiress

As I'm trying on huge bug-eyed sunglasses . . .

MOM: You look like Parrot Houston.

ME: Who? . . . Oh, Paris Hilton?!?

many more

My mom and I are watching *A Walk to Remember* . . .

MOM: You know, her mom really named her well.

ME: Who?

MOM: Many More.

ME: What?

MOM: Many More! She's a good actress so I want to see Many More of her!

ME: You mean MANDY Moore??

finding emo

ME: Hey, Mom, do you know what "emo" means?

MOM: Yes.

ME: Really? **(not expecting that response)**

MOM: Ya . . . it's a fish.

ME: What?

MOM: YOU KNOW **(looks at me as if I'm completely stupid)** . . . *Finding Emo!*

inappropriate touching

MOM: Why is Eminem controversial? Is it because he's a white guy who acts black?

ME: I dunno. Some people think he's misogynistic.

MOM: What? **(looks really offended)**

ME: It means that he hates women.

MOM (still offended): Why would you say something like that to me?

ME: Misogynistic? I know it's not a common word, but I explained what it meant.

MOM: Why would you say in front of your mother that he's . . . **(flustered)** massaging his dick?!

destiny's child gets thirsty

MOM: Why are they singing "lemonade, lemonade"?

ME: It's "Say my name, say my name . . ."

musical interpretations

Huey's "Pop, Lock & Drop It" plays on the radio . . .

MOM: Why do you listen to this? It's terrible.

ME: It's not that bad.

MOM: What are they saying, "Stop blocking traffic"?

ME: Yes. That's what they're saying.

mythical mix-up

MOM: Are you going to watch *Nightlight*?

ME: Um, what?

MOM: *Nightlight*. You know, it just beat the Larry Porrey* books.

ME: . . . Do you mean *Twilight*? Probably not.

---

* Harry Potter

MOM: Yes, *Nightlight*. Why not? I remember you like vampire shows, like Buddy.

ME: Mom, it's Buffy, not Buddy.

MOM: Same things. You know what I mean.

fruity salesmen

MOM: You should eat everything here. Make you strong like Papaya.

ME (looking around for papaya and not finding any): Huh?

MOM: You know . . . they have a song, "Papaya the Salesman."

ME: Um . . . Popeye the Sailor Man?

black men on tv

ME: Ma, these steaks are amazing!

BROTHER: Mmmm, so good, wow . . . thanks, Ma!

MOM: Yes, and my grill is so great because it drips excess oil while it's grilling the meat! Simple and easy to clean, and keeps us healthier. I bought one for your Aunt Jean in Taiwan, too, since it's so handy. I just love my Morgan Freeman Grill!

(my brother and I look at each other, confused)

BROTHER: Ma . . . did you mean . . . your George Fore man Grill?

MOM: You two always like to pick at my English. Their names are similar, OK? And they're both nice black men I see on TV!

slutoween

MOM: we'r going to martin's halloween party this wkend

MOM: We are going as pip and pip's girl, so we can reuse the costums for our wine bar's halloween party, they have the theme of 70s and 80s

ME: who is pip?

MOM: I mean pinp, is that how u spell?

ME: a pimp?

ME: like a pimp and a prostitute . . . ?

MOM: yes

ME: ok . . . that is kind of scandalous?

MOM: why

ME: bc that would make u a prostitute!

ME: (or a "ho")

MOM: well . . . we already got the costumes

MOM: should check w u first

ME: i cant believe dad is ok with that

MOM: his idea

injecting buttocks

While watching an entertainment show . . .

ME: There is no way that man is 50! He looks 25!

MOM: You know they are actors and actresses. They cover
up their wrinkles with that buttocks stuff.

ME: What? Buttocks?

MOM: Buttocks, Botox, same thing.

the sound of sirens

Nas's "One Mic" was playing in the background . . .

MOM: Oh my god! (she pulls over)

ME: Why the hell did you just pull over?

MOM: Don't you hear the fire truck sound? It's coming!
(turns off radio) Oh . . . HAHAHA . . . American
music is so strange . . .

shake, shake it!

MOM: I've been watching dance videos to learn how to dance.

ME: What dances?

MOM: Tango, salsa, cha-cha-cha . . . that way I will be ready at your wedding.

ME: Mom, I'll only have hip hop.

MOM: I can do that, too! Aerobics class taught me to just shake my hips a lot.

phone calls from mario land

My mom and I were talking about bad grades I earned in elementary school . . .

MOM: You did so bad in school the Super Nintendo called me to speak to me!

when disney characters say "om"

My mom and I had taken a yoga class earlier in the day and
were driving past Disneyland . . .

MOM: What is Donald Duck?

ME: Huh?

MOM: Donald Duck?

ME: Oh, Mickey Mouse's friend. You know . . . the duck?

MOM: Then why did the instructor keep telling us to do
Donald Duck?

ME: . . . Huh?

MOM: You know, when you bend over on the mat . . .

ME: Downward dog?

dirty games

MOM: Hey, you want to bring your *Playboy*?

ME: My what?

MOM: I mean . . . your boy toy.

ME: . . .

MOM: You know, the game that you take with you.

ME: Oh! Gameboy!

punch buggy fail

My sister and I were playing punch buggy in the backseat of the car (in which you punch somebody else in the car every time you see a Volkswagen Beetle) . . .

MOM (to my dad): What are they doing? I told them no violence!

DAD: No, no, it's a game they play where you hit if you see a type of car.

MOM: Ooh, I see . . .

MOM: Chevrolet! **(hits my dad)**

ME: No, Mommy, you don't get to pick what kind, it's a specific car!

MOM: Oh, OK. I get it!

(moments later)

MOM: BMW!? **(hits my dad)**

band name perversion

I had been single for quite some time so my mom confronted me about my credit card statement . . .

MOM: I saw your credit card statement and one entry had "Fall Out Boy" for $80.

ME: Yeah, so?

MOM: Are you calling gay sex hotline?

ME: They are tickets for a concert!

rubbing in the loss

The USC Trojans steamrollered my Cal Bears at our home-coming game, 30–3. My mom knew I went to the game, and the following night, she messaged me on Facebook . . .

MOM: my dear

ME: yes mother

MOM: the Bear lost to Trojan

ME: i was there mother

MOM: big loss

ME: i was there mother but thank you for reminding me

MOM: Trojan seems to be very powerful

MOM: looks like private college have an upper hand

MOM: UCLA lost to Stanford

cold music

My mom and I were driving to lunch as I played some music in my car really low . . .

MOM: You can turn it louder if you want.

ME: You don't like this music, Mom.

MOM: Yes, I do.

ME: No, you don't. It's rap.

MOM: I like the rap. Who is that? Ice cream?

ME: No, his name is Ice Cube.

MOM: Yeah, I like the Ice Cube and ice cream together!

asian mom's tribute to michael jackson

I walked into the living room one day and found my mom standing in front of the coffee table shuffling her feet. She was staring intently at her laptop screen with what appeared to be a YouTube exercise tutorial playing in the background. I asked her what she was doing, and she responded proudly, "The moonwalk!"

from god to gangsters

When I was in sixth grade, I walked into the living room while my mother was watching a movie. She looked at me, horrified . . .

> **MOM:**   What kind of movie is this?
>
> **ME:**   It's *The Godfather*—Mom, this movie is really violent. It's about gangsters.
>
> **MOM:**   It's not about God?
>
> **ME:**   No, Mom, that's God THE Father. This is THE Godfather.

talking food

We were in the car listening to "Say" by John Mayer . . .

> **MOM:**   "Sandwich you need to say, sandwich you need to say."
>
> **ME:**   . . . Sandwich? Don't you mean "Say what you need to say"? You have to listen to it more carefully!
>
> **MOM (turns it up louder):** . . . SEE, IT'S SANDWICH!

i like this. (thumbs up!)

This was my aunt's Facebook status . . .

> **Hong L** just saw the movie Fast and Furious, cool!!! Paul
> is so hot. How the hell they found so many hot girls in
> that movie . . . no FAT chicks at all.

like cantaloupe

We turned on the Oscars to see who won Best Supporting
Actress . . .

MOM: Oh, look!

US: What?

MOM: It's Peneloupe Cruz! I love her acting.

US: Penelope?

MOM: No, it's Peneloupe. Can't you read?

baha men move to hong kong

A song was playing on the radio . . .

MOM: They like to sing about left hand? What is coo?

ME: What?

MOM: They sing, "Coo ley goh joh suw."*

ME: OH! "Who let the dogs out?!"

rappers are millionaires anyway

"Whatever You Like" by TI was playing on the radio . . .

MOM: Is this from Slumdog?

ME: No. *Slumdog Millionaire* didn't have rapping.

MOM: You know, Slumdog . . . **(then, with emphasis)** Slooooom-dog?

ME: . . . Do you mean SNOOP Dogg??

MOM: Oh, yeah, whatever, the rapper! Snoop means smelling, right?

my imaginary pet dragon

ME: Hey, Mom, do you want to go see *How to Train Your Dragon*?

---

* In Cantonese, that sounds like "Coo your left hand."

MOM: Why? I don't have dragon!?

ME: Mom, it's a movie . . .

MOM: So? I still don't have dragon!

24-hour jack-packed action

I made my mom a Facebook profile a few months ago. After watching the season premiere of *24,* she updated her Facebook status . . .

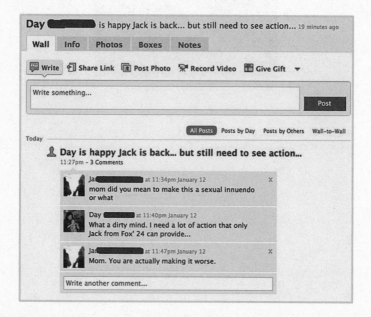

guitar heroine

rock band talent

the new mac dre

CHAPTER TEN

why we still love them

Maybe they make blatantly racist comments about people who are within earshot, and the love advice they dish isn't always the soundest. Anyone who has endured the marathonesque rigor of growing up in a fobby mother's household deserves all the steamed pork buns the world has to offer. But regardless of their no-holds-barred criticism of our thunder thighs, their inability to understand why we just can't date their church friend's electrical engineering computer science IBM-bound son, and their insistence on wearing plastic welder hats in public, we love our fobby moms—and unconditionally so. It's because of—or perhaps in spite of—everything they say and do that we have a sneaking suspicion that maybe, just maybe . . . they love us right back.

advice, meaningful quotes, and declarations of love

Dear Alex,

Happy EASTER DAY!

Some info share with you.

1)—-NOTH CAN STOP THE MAN WITH THE RIGHT MENTAL ATTITUDE FROM A CHIEVING HAS GOAL. NOTHING ON EARTH CAN HELP THE MAN WITH THE WRONG ATTITUDE.—-THOMAS JEFFERSON—-

2)—NOTHING IS GOOD OR BAD BUT OUR THINKING MAKE IT SO.—-SHAKESPEARE—-

3)—WE MUST DO THE BEST WE CAN WITH WHAT WE HAVE.—-EDWARD ROWLANDSILL—

4)—IF YOU DON'T LIKE SOMETHING, CHANGE IT, IF YOU CAN'T CHANGE IT, CHANGE YOUR ALLITUDE, DON'T COMPLAIN.—-MAYA ANGELOU—-

5)—YOU MAY DELAY, BUT TIME WILL NOT.–FORLANKERLIN—

6) Bill Gtes likes asks a questions when he interview youth for job.

HOW WOULD YOU MOVE FUJI MOUNTAIN?

Bill Gates said the question is no answear, he wondering understand How are the Youth thinking.

Did you read a book Name "HOW WOULD YOU MOVE FUJI"?

I love you forever
Mom

killing the squirrel

Dear Princess,

I would like to write you some keys to better driving notes from Han's work book. Approach to Driving is built upon four undeerlying concepts:

1. As a driver you need effective seeing habbits. Ninety percent of the information you use to drive comes through your eyes. The Collisionfree! Approach to Driving provides simple techniques to help you use your vision to its greatest effect. This will allow you time to process what you see.

2. You must maintain space in which to operate your vechicle,. You need space in front, behind and whenever possible, on both sides. This space allows you to see

effectively and provides you with an escape route in case of trouble.

3. All other road users need space too. You must time your maneuver in traffic, especially when entering the flow or changinjg lanes, to avoid taking away another driver's space, forcing them to brake or take evasive action.,

4. Finally, in the Collisionfree!Approach to Driving we take the position that prevention is better than cure. You must strive to drive proactively. You will attempt to predict the actions of other road users and then act before they do to avoid conflict. Ninety-five percent of the Collisionfree!Approach to Driving is proactive.

These four concepts are supported by habbits and sub-habbits. Habbits are behaviours that have been repoeated so often that they are now done without any conscious thought.

Habbit 1: Look Well Ahead

Habbit 2: Move Your Eyes

Habbit 3: Keep Space

Habbit 4: Spot the Problems

Do not jeopardize human life to avoid a small animal.

Please read and review these 4 habits.

Love Mommy, XOXO

translation: come home, please

I still have your mooncakes lying by the door. Maybe I
need to put them in the frig. :-(Lonely Mooncakes!

on behalf of the dog

i'm boring! when will y come back to play with me?
i have been 5 pus a day, how about y? i have dinner
already, see y soon.—dylin

laptop is ill

Do not look for me after 3pm. I need to pick up my
repaired laptop—my laptop fall sick during the break
most probably due to missing all of U. Now its smiling
and I need to pick it back.

All the best for your midterm and happy mugging!

laundry list

This is a handwritten note Mom left on the refrigerator door for us (ages 27, 26, and 23) before she and my dad left for a trip to China . . .

Trash day on Tuestday. (Put out the trash on Monday night, Make sure to wash your hands after you touch the trash can.)

Change towels in the kitchen everyday and the one in the powderoom often.

Wash dishes when it gets full. Fill up the Liquet in both cups. Better wash at night, remember to pull them out before you go to sleep, let them airdry all night before you unload them the next day. Takes about an hour to wash.

Whipe the toilet and bathroom floor often.

Use my cell phone to call me often. China numbers are on the frige door. We are 12 hours diffrent.

Eat vegetables and fruit everyday.

Cut the grass when they get tall.

Check the answer machine often. (It is in our bedroom.)

Empty the trash can in the kitchen often.

Water the plants often includes the one in the masterbedroom bathroom (don't water too much on this one because there are no holes in the bottom of the pot.)

There are more toilet pappers and tissues in the guestroom closet.

There are frozen soups from last time still in the freezer.

Check the freezer and frige down the basement and the kitchen before you cook. There food everywhere includes the freezer in the garage.

You need milk and bread soon.

Thank you!

Take care yourself. Take care each other. Take care the house. See you soon. Love you! Miss you!

all my children

Dear Children's

We are finally moved ! what I mean is at least we are moved all belonging to one place.

We don't know how long will take organize but at least we do not have to wary two or three place.

We are very much appreciate you guys concern and support for this events.

Even you were not with us physically I know you were concern us and supportive.

We do like to say thank you for that.

Bye and have good days.

self-congratulatory greeting card

My birthday card from my parents looked very fancy, with a ribbon and everything, until I opened it . . .

Our son a result of good parenting.

Signed,
Mom and Dad.

sweet-and-sour 20th birthday

Dear Sophia, Happy 20th Birthday!

The poem of this card describes exactly what we want to express to our dearest daughter on her 20th birthday! raising a girl to an adolescence, is a journey of ups-and-downs, sweet-and-sour but a rewarding experience. Dad and I are so proud to have you and you're always our #1 priority! May you dare to dream, to persevere, and succeed and be happy always!

. . . P.S. 20th birthday for girls is very import to Chinese parents. My parents gave me the jade bracelet that I wore over 27 years—it has been my daily companion in happy times, in hardship when i was pioneer in USA, in failure and in success. so we chose this. . . .

tuff times when you were litter

Karen: Did you remember when you litter, I have to get up 5:30 am and 6:30 am in the car to Cerritos, those were tuff time, but good memory. hope this Sunday we go shopping together, I pay for everything. Including nonsense.

Please e-mail me back all the time, then I can practice my English. Otherwise my English getting worse. See you. Bye

late-night revelations

Hi John,

I have watched the DVD that really gives me more release and comfort. I feel much better now.

When you first told me on the street, my heart was shaking and full of pain, yet, I didn't show it to you as I do not want to let you know that I was shocked.

When I know you are a gay, right away I have been thinking the sex, nothing else. That's why I always ask who is the woman? After watching the DVD, I realize that besides sex, there is "LOVE"; sharing love, sharing the popcorn, sorrow and joy, sharing both families, sharing tears and laughter, sharing buildings, delicious food, traveling etc. I FOUND THAT YOU ARE IN LOVE WITH HAPPINESS. Now I can let it go as your other-side cares and loves you so much.

God condemns the sin, but not the sinner. I am relieved.

Good night.

Mom

nice picture for happy family

In response to a picture message I sent of her grandson in his
dinosaur Halloween costume . . .

> Oky doky! Thank you so much. Oh my god! It is very
> nice picture. He is so cute n so lovely. Now he is a dino-
> saur. I got some clothes for you. I may drop it off.
> Thank you so much for sending me nice new picture.
> Very pretty. I am so happy with your family. Bye. Umma. . . .

ain't no mountain

> Sophia,
>
> When I return to Fremont, count on me, I am your rock
> and your unfailing support all the time, because I am
> your cheerleader.
> I know and I am prepared to support you during this
> very difficult time. But, that's life. When you have a goal,
> when you have a high mountain to climb up, this is a nec-
> essary process. In the future, in life, you will encounter
> the same journey. I have been in your shoes many times

in my life. You have seen me ups and downs. but our family is always a harbor for us to rest in the evening, to depart for our goal in the early morning.

Mom

guardian angel

Received in the middle of the night . . .

when you pass through waters, I will be with you and when you pass through the rivers, they will not sweep over you. when you walk through the fire, you will not be burned,the flames will not set you ablaze. you are mine. good nite~

reach for the stars

The firm that I interviewed with decided to rescind their offer. I called my mom and she gave me a pep talk. Afterward, she sent me this text . . .

if one door closed try find another. still have window. still have roof. push them u will see the sky. sky is

unlimited so are u. never lose your faith. not u. ur my
chinese girl. love mom.

forecast warning

sno storm tonite dont get too drunk and die on the street.

confucian proverbs

dearest jasmine,

please try to have a nice posture, stand high as mountain, root your feet to the ground as tree, express your
beauty through kindness and wisdom,
   you are amazing person, i love you.

you are my sunshine

Response to an email regarding a pimple . . .

Yes. It will be go away. Don't cry for pimple~ ~ ~. You
will smile tomorrow ~ ~.

Mom

tips from a karaoke pro

How to practice:

First listen original music until memories full melody, then sing alone with original song together by looking lyrics. Then finally, you sing by karaoke melody.

Mom

best present ever

Hi!

I just received your new Driver License! It will expire in 2014! Wow!

Mom Just bought a BLENDTEC machine and it is wonderful.

I am thinking about buy you two girls one each.

This machine is so powerful and so easy to make healthy smoothie, soup, soybean milk, ...

You can go to the internet and view the demo and reviews about this machine. (google with "blendtec")

Even though it is very expensive ($411 after tax at Costco with a 7 years warranty), but it will last and the health benefit for you is priceless.

How about have this as a early "Wedding" present?

lol (I just learned what this means)

The promotion ends next week.

Let me know soon!

Love,

hi girl ^_^

Hi Girl,

I know you are busy today, I believe you have to go to the bank, and school ect..and some things else. Remember Email your phone number and your address.I going to buy a card tomorrow then call you. How are you recently? tell me every things it does not matter good or bad, happy or sad. ☺ ☻ ☺ bad, also remember carry this ☂ with you.

Oh! how is my English? Grammar? correct me.

Mom

dramatic drinks

My mom emailed me after we had a huge fight . . .

> Ok, you will be fine for everthing. Actually you are excel-
> lent so far. I will support you for all. you are my only
> child. it is not the big deal. I will help you. We need the
> drama in life. Otherwise the lift will only like the water.
> We need the different drink. ok? take care. go to sleep.

big-breasted snowman

It snowed a ton in New York not too long ago, and my mom,
who is from California, had this to say about me making a
snowman, via her new favorite form of communication, text
message . . .

MOM: Exciting! Try to make a female snowman!
ME: Will do mom
MOM: Take a picture of it! Make sure the cup size is 40
DDD!

candy chomp, chomp!

Hi Elizabeth,

How are you doing? How is your paper coming along? I miss you~~~~. How are you surviving the below freezing weather in Boston? It's so cold here, too, with the temperature hovering around 38 F~. I am very sleepy at work, staring at & trying to read these boring scientific progress reports—. Only thing I can do is eat MORE chocolates. I have Christmas colored peanut M&Ms, mini 3 Musketeers mint dark chocolate, mini Twix bars & Dove mint silky milk chocolate squares~~~. I also had those mint M&M, but I ate them all—gobbled them down—chomp, chomp!.

I hope you are not following my example and be good, eating healthy snacks. ;)

Love you & miss you.

Love,
Mom

fish metaphors

Why do you post "boston deal of a day" everyday? It is
so boring. Please do not do it anymore. Don't you have a
midterm in this week? When you finish your midterm you
should finish Boston university and Tufts secondary application, because they are in Boston area, it is easy to go
interviewing. You do not need to book ticket and hotel.

Now, you are like a salmon in the ocean trying to
swim bravely and courageously to the upper stream
accomplishing your mission.

Best wishes
Mom

a refitgisrator afterthought

Dear Kids

Dad & MOM are going to vacation, Please take good
care of yourself. Drive safe & go home early, when you
are cooking don't forget to turn the stove off, keep
check all the door before going out & sleep. of course
don't forget PRETZEL he need all of you to love & give

him food & water . . . OH..oh..OH..ohhhhhhh.. . . . I L O
V E YOUUUuuuuUUUUuuuuUUUUuuu too (need food
check the refitgisrator I had food to feed you).
  I LOVE YOU

Lovely
M O M

self-confidence is key!

MOM: Listen! I got my hair done n look fabulous!
ME: haha yay! Whats it look like now?
MOM: Hot

if you give a girl a cookie . . . 😲

From: Me

is there any way you can mail me royal bakery cookies? i
miss them ☹

From: Mom

How many cookies do you want? I can priority mail
them. It only takes two days. No problem. I'll put them

in a zip lock bag. Better let me know now. I'm about to leave at 9am. I'm waiting for your answer. I'm sitting right here at the computer.

love, mama

#1 mom's first email ☺

Hi ! Daughter ,

Thank you for the Birthday gift .

We were enjoy it. I try call you before but I think you were busy . . .

So what are you doing now ?

I know you so busy today . House working , eating good food for week(?) , watching movie . . . talking (or sweet thing ~~???) with #1 your man ☺

Here , all family is OK . . .

My daughter , "Have a wonderful weekend !!" with your #1 man !

Love , mom .

roomba jetson

MOM: oh i am so happy

ME: why, what'd you do

MOM: rosy is doing such a good job. she doesn't complain or talk to me, or get in the way. when i am in the room, she just avoids me and keeps cleaning. she cleans all day!

ME: you hired a maid?

MOM: i bought one!

ME: um. how did you do that?

MOM: i got rosy!!

ME: i dont think you can just buy people

MOM: you know from the jetsons? that's my favorite show when i come to usa.

ME: i dont know what you are talking about. i need to go.

Another day . . .

MOM: i got you robot maid. her name is lucy. because i already have rosy

ME: why lucy?

MOM: because i have rosy

My mom got me a Roomba, too.

think positive thoughts

Here's my mom in an effort to make me look on the bright side . . .

MOM: Well, how is your mint plant doing?

ME: It died.

MOM: That's wonderful, darling! It died to give you life, the yin and the yang.

lolspeak

Dear Felicia:

How are you doing? Back to school always exited, right ? say hi to your lovely girl freinds and all those sticky boys for me lol ,ahhh, i like this word lol, it looks like somebody hands a ball to me. Capital LOL likes people are kicking a ball. Lol like a ball find a hole to

slip away from cage (this is what i feel when i drove you
to airport), lOl looks like I am squeezing Chang Yi's
cheeks. IOL Ahhh.. . . . . . . I am leaning on a comfortable
cushion.. . . . . . ahhhhhhh . .. .

Love,
Mom

sin city dangers

Mike,

I heard you will go to Las Vegas for a Bachelor party.
I concern of the event.

One should consider himself with Dignity in Respect-
ful manner. Reckless people might want to put you in
Test. Specially while you're in toxic(alcohol), suggesting
you to do some activities that you shouldn't ever do, like
sleeping with a dangerous girl.

When I mentioned my concerns to Simmons, he told
me about [Hang over] movie. I'm not sure what is about
that movie, but keep in mind that Marriage is one step
of Maturity process to become responsible in order to
make a Family unit, which include a child. So don't get
tricked by less sincere people's attempt to ruin your life.

Enjoy your life as mush, but always remind yourself that you have a wide awakened conscious is observing you to guide you in Light to make you eventually an Enlighten one.

I trust you always, but because of my caution I had to mention this.

with great love,
Mom

chopstick knitting

My mom proudly told me about how, when she found out knitting needles weren't allowed on a plane, she decided to modify chopsticks instead. Not going to let rules against sharp objects get in the way of her in-flight activities . . .

is it food or fake boobs?

My mom was with her best friend, and they were playing with Taiwanese food, *ba-wan*. They both laughed when my sister said that *ba-wan*s looked like silicone implants with tumors in them . . .

welcome home!

I always come home from school for winter and summer breaks.
My mom and grandma like to make me feel welcome . . .

happy family in sun shine day

My mom was complaining about the pile of stuffed animals
I had sitting on the corner of my dresser, and decided to dust
them off and put them in the porch to sun for a while because
they were getting musty. Then she decided to take pictures
and send them to the entire extended family . . .

Jennifer has 26 babies. They are either beanny or
puffy, tiny or huge, cuty or scary, fancy or simply. She
just wants to keep them even now she is a medical

school student. Specially the beanny cow which is the
first beanny baby she got from grandma.

Today is a sun shine day. I brought all her babies
to the porch to get the sun and fresh air.

What a big and happy family!

frowny frog

victory cactus

christmas plant

My mom and her (economical) Christmas tree . . .

dual-purpose card

My mom wanted to give me a card before my move to New York. She had this one lying around . . .

ME: Mom, this is a business card about financial investment!

MOM: Well . . . we talk about your Roth IRA?

Dear Mel,   9-25-09
Be strong & Courageous Do Not be
terrified; do not be discouraged.
for the Lord your God will be with
You wherever you go.
    Joshua 1:9
        Love Mom
God Be With You & Bless You always

Thank you for the opportunity to
discuss your financial plans.

I look forward to working with you.

Your Personal Imprint Appears Here.
(Up to four lines at prices shown)

when i weak up in the morning

My younger brother was off from school for a week, so he slept in. Before I got back from class, my mom called me to say that my younger brother was going out, so she left him a note asking him to call her about his plans for the day.

I looked in his room but didn't see a note, not in the hallway, nor in the kitchen. He eventually called her, and I eventually found the note . . .